Paul Scholes

The Biography

SIMON MOSS

Paul Scholes

The Biography

JOHN BLAKE

Published by John Blake Publishing Ltd,
3 Bramber Court, 2 Bramber Road,
London W14 9PB, England

www.johnblakepublishing.co.uk

First published in hardback in 2009

ISBN: 978-1-84454-747-0

British Library Cataloguing-in-Publication Data:

A catalogue record for this book is available from the British Library.

Design by www.envydesign.co.uk

All inside photography © Clevamedia

Printed in Great Britain by CPI William Clowes Ltd, Beccles, NR34 7TL

1 3 5 7 9 10 8 6 4 2

Papers used by John Blake Publishing are natural, recyclable products made from wood
grown in sustainable forests. The manufacturing processes conform to the environmental
regulations of the country of origin.

Every attempt has been made to contact the relevant copyright-holders, but some were
unobtainable. We would be grateful if the appropriate people could contact us.

CONTENTS

Chapter 1

FERGIE'S FLEDGLINGS

'To miss the biggest club game in the world must be
hard to take. But Scholes didn't let it destroy him, because
he has achieved so much.'

SIR ALEX FERGUSON

When Peter Schmeichel and Sir Alex Ferguson held the Champions League trophy aloft that memorable night in Barcelona they lifted more than forty years of history that had weighed so heavily on the Manchester United side each time they performed in Europe. It was poignant that their long overdue triumph fell on the 90th birthday of Sir Matt Busby, the mastermind of United's only previous win in the competition and the man who brought the club back from the abyss to be crowned Kings of Europe in just a decade.

Paul Scholes stood a subdued bystander as his teammates celebrated their breathtaking victory in Barcelona's 'cathedral of football', the Nou Camp. He was forced to sit out the defining moment of Ferguson's twenty-year reign at the helm of

Manchester United, with suspension ruling him out of the game following a mistimed challenge in the semi-final triumph over Turin giants Juventus.

'To miss the biggest club game in the world must be hard to take,' Ferguson had said. 'But Scholes didn't let it destroy him, because he has achieved so much.'

In a season when the Red Devils were famed for doing things the hard way, the loss of Scholes and midfield partner Roy Keane to suspension decimated Ferguson's side ahead of the most important match for nearly half a century, making the task of overcoming a battle hardened Bayern Munich all the more difficult. David Beckham slotted into central midfield alongside Nicky Butt, with Jesper Blomqvist given a rare chance to shine on the greatest stage in club football.

The weight of expectation that travels with Ferguson's Reds each time they perform in Europe is always suffocating and it reached its climax as the team lined up alongside their German counterparts in the Catalan capital. The spectre of United's tragic past casts an imposing shadow over any player who pulls on the famous red jersey. Not since the days of George Best, Bobby Charlton and Denis Law had Manchester United enjoyed such success and, fittingly, their dominance was based on players brought through the youth system. The comparisons between the Ferguson and Busby eras cannot be ignored. The history of Manchester United Football Club will show that a careful nurturing of youth reaps the biggest rewards.

So, when Ole Gunnar Solskjaer steered the ball into the roof of the net in the 93rd minute, he brought to an end the greatest odyssey in British football history. The baby-faced assassin netted the crucial goal to secure the historic treble of Premier League, FA Cup and Champions League.

While the celebrations went on long into the night in the city of Barcelona, for Ferguson the evening had capped nearly a decade of planning, nurturing and patience.

Many great players have defined the Ferguson era in the history of Manchester United Football Club. Eric Cantona, Roy Keane and Peter Schmeichel are a few who have helped bring unprecedented success to the Red Devils, usurping bitter rivals Liverpool to stand at the summit of English football. But it is the team of youngsters, carefully brought through from raw talent into first-team regulars, who have been the backbone of the club during the most successful spell Old Trafford has ever enjoyed.

Paul Scholes, a Salford-born midfielder, has been an integral part of Alex Ferguson's side for well over a decade, winning eight Premier League titles, three FA Cups, the Intercontinental Cup and of course the Champions League – twice. He has often been considered an unappreciated member of the Manchester United side, but his opponents are all too aware of the damage Paul Scholes can cause when given even the smallest opportunity.

The Old Trafford faithful granted him the title of the 'Ginger Prince' to King Eric Cantona and it was alongside the French maestro that Scholes would establish himself as indispensable to Ferguson. International football soon came calling for Scholes, who won his first England cap in the landmark friendly against South Africa in 1997 and earned a place in England's World Cup squad in 1998 (see Chapter 9, 'England International').

Ever devoted to his beloved Reds, he retired from international football at just 29 to concentrate on domestic issues – and, importantly, his young family – at a time when Arsenal and Chelsea began to flex their muscles in the Premier League. During his brief tenure as England boss, Steve McClaren tried to lure Scholes out of his international retirement when it became clear that England's midfield needed an order and presence that only Scholes could offer the national coach. He duly declined, and Manchester United have reaped the rewards of one of the greatest midfield stars of a generation.

I

Scholes was a member of the Manchester United youth team in the early 1990s, a squad that is sure to become the stuff of legend. With British football coming under heavy criticism for its increasing reliance on foreign imports, the Reds' homegrown stars were a breath of fresh air throughout a turbulent first decade for the new Premier League. The same Manchester United youth team unleashed Scholes, David Beckham, Ryan Giggs, Nicky Butt and the Neville brothers on the unsuspecting Premiership, with all going on to collect their Champions League winners' medals in Barcelona seven years later. It is an astonishing achievement that few academies will ever be able to boast.

Being a part of Manchester United Football Club means you must immerse yourself in over a century of success, glory and tragedy. It is a club that has endured more than any other, and continues to raise the bar and fight off all who challenge its dominance of English football. The Busby Babes set a precedent for all who would follow them and, under Sir Alex Ferguson, Manchester United have been able to bring back the glory days first enjoyed by Busby and his fledgling stars, so tragically brought down in their prime. As Roy Keane said in his autobiography, 'Even the greatest players, the most hardened professionals, would never be indifferent to, or immune from, the history of the club. Living with the demands imposed by the history was a constant challenge, the constant challenge of being a Manchester United player.'

The Busby Babes have never left the collective conscious of Manchester United and are immortalised at Old Trafford, where more than 75,000 fanatics keep their memory alive. To be part of a Manchester United youth team brings a certain responsibility when looking at the players who have graduated from the class.

Roy Keane acknowledges the pressure faced by any Manchester United footballer: 'Matt Busby, Bobby Charlton, George Best, Denis Law, the Munich team. Because of them I wanted to play for United. They are the reason why wherever Manchester United play there is a buzz of expectation. It's a tall order. Every time I pull on a red shirt I'm conscious of the responsibility of being a United player.'

Busby was an innovator. A man who rebuilt a team deeply wounded by the Munich air disaster into European Champions in just a decade, it was his policy on youth that Ferguson reaffirmed when he took the reigns at Old Trafford in 1986.

Busby once said, 'If you want football's finest roots, you grow your own'. And it was with this philosophy that Ferguson built his team of champions. All of Manchester United's top five appearance-makers have come from the youth team. Bobby Charlton, Ryan Giggs, Bill Foulkes, Gary Neville and Scholes all rose through the ranks at Old Trafford. Charlton, perhaps Manchester United's greatest ever servant, paid tribute to Scholes, who he feels perfectly encapsulates everything a Manchester United player should be. 'I love watching Paul Scholes,' he said. 'He is an absolute credit. He is so professional and so good that, when he gets the ball, I get a real satisfaction. I say, "This will not be wasted." And, sure enough, the number of times he picks the ball up, the direction of his passing, the quality of his passing, the way that he can find time on the ball – it's an instinctive thing and it is such a pleasure to watch'.

Charlton admits he finds it difficult to believe that he is the same player he first watched as a youth two decades ago.

'I can't believe that he is in his thirties. I still think of him as the little lad at sixteen, seventeen that I saw in a youth match in Sunderland all those years ago. We were four up in twenty minutes and I thought, "Wow, we've got some players here." And it was all the players who came through. Nicky Butt, the Nevilles, David Beckham, Ryan Giggs, Paul Scholes – and Paul is still there, and he's still one of the best passers in the game'.

Scholes and Charlton draw instant comparisons. Both shunned the limelight of celebrity in favour of a more modest and dignified existence outside football, though on the pitch they were tough, uncompromising and successful. Charlton was the ever-present hero of the Busby era of Manchester United Football Club, and it was Busby who launched Duncan Edwards – regarded by many as the finest English talent ever – into the Manchester United first team, and much of his success and plaudits came from his faith in youth and in grooming young, raw talent into champions. The Reds won the FA Youth Cup, so often the marker of success at that level, for the first five years of its existence. These players earned the right to feature in the first team and Busby duly obliged. This brought Manchester United great success during the 1950s and 1960s and continues to be the policy today.

Ferguson admits he is delighted that the youth team of the early 1990s have been the foundation of his all-conquering side for nearly two decades. 'Ryan Giggs, Gary Neville and Paul Scholes are the heartbeat of the team,' he said. 'They have all been here since they were thirteen. They are in their thirties now and I don't think there's another team anywhere that has three players who have been around for getting on twenty years. It's fantastic, absolutely amazing.

'I think it's important for a club like United to have a Mancunian heartbeat,' he continued.

But not only this: Ferguson hopes the loyalty and commitment shown by Scholes will prove to the club's second generation of young superstars that they can fulfil all their dreams at Old Trafford.

'Wayne Rooney and Cristiano Ronaldo, for example, see Ryan, Gary and Paul,' Ferguson explained. 'They see how contented they all are and it must give them confidence to know they're at the right club.'

Ferguson instigated a thorough overhaul of Manchester United's youth system when he arrived from Aberdeen in 1986, insisting that only the best local talent would be granted a place in the Centre of Excellence. This restructuring included a change in staffing, with United legend Brian Kidd coming in as director of the Centre of Excellence. Kidd was himself a product of United's youth team of the 1960s which included Scottish prodigy Arthur Albiston, the giant South African goalkeeper Gary Bailey and the mercurial George Best. But a major coup for Ferguson in building his team of fledgling stars was the snatching of Ryan Wilson from the clutches of Manchester City. Wilson – in the days before he took his mother's name of Giggs – had established himself as one of the hottest prospects in European football and his arrival heralded an influx of local talent into United's youth system.

One such player was Paul Scholes, born at Hope Hospital in Salford to parents Stewart and Marina on 16 November 1974 – the same year Manchester United triumphed in the second division under Scottish tactician Tommy Docherty. It was a pivotal season for United, bouncing back to the top tier of English football at the first time of asking aided by Lou Macari, Stewart Houston and Brian Greenhoff – the players who were brought in to replace the old guard of Denis Law, George Best and Bobby Charlton as United moved away from the legendary era under Busby.

At only 18 months old, the infant Scholes moved to the Langley Estate of Middleton, Greater Manchester, on the banks of the River Irk. It was here that Scholes would develop the skills that would one day lead him to the farthest corners of the globe for club and country. The streets of Langley – as in the eyes of all youngsters – became the hallowed turf of Wembley, and thus, by his own admission, Scholes enjoyed a tentative relationship with the neighbours. However, few would have realised the prospects of the player who had begun to flourish on the streets of Langley, as the Ginger Prince began took his first steps towards football's greatest royalties.

The young Scholes attended St Mary's Roman Catholic Primary School in Langley, where he played in his first competitive football matches for the school team as the fledgling superstar got his first taste of competitive action on a football field. Showing an obvious flair and aptitude at such a young age, Scholes joined Langley Furrow – a collection of youngsters playing local football in Middleton. While these early forays into competitive football may not have brought unmitigated success, they formed a crucial part of the development of Paul Scholes as a footballer.

At age 11 he moved to Cardinal Langley Secondary School, where his talent started to draw the attention of scouts across Greater Manchester. During an interview with BBC Radio Manchester, Scholes confessed that school never held much appeal to him, and was merely the means by which he could access sport, where he continued to excel. 'I was never great at school', he confessed. 'I never enjoyed doing the work and all the homework. I just went to play football, cricket or whatever sport I could play. Fortunately, Cardinal Langley had a very good reputation and was a good school for sport.'

As the star of the team, Scholes helped Cardinal Langley win the Catholic Cup – the local tournament for school sports teams – five years running and enhanced his own reputation as a potential star in the making.

Scholes played for Boundary Park Juniors, where he met some of Lancashire's best footballing talent of the time, and his former coach can barely contain his delight at having played his part in the development of some of England's greatest stars.

'Paul was the first to join us,' Mike Walsh – a shop fitter and former Boundary Park coach – told the *Sunday Mirror*. 'He was so small it was like picking a baby. But that didn't stop him scoring eight goals in one game, every one with his head. I used to play him on the right wing, but he loved scoring goals so much he'd always drift towards to the centre-forward position. The boy was amazingly skilful, but I had to leave him out of the team for his own safety at times. He was up against kids twice his size and they could get quite nasty.'

He grew up supporting his father's team, Oldham Athletic, and claims Andy Ritchie as his hero. The Manchester-born star netted 82 goals for Athletic between 1987 and 1995, and it says a lot about Scholes that, despite the wealth of footballing talent around in his youth, he grew up idolising a home-grown player over the likes of Diego Maradona, Michel Platini and Johan Cruyff.

'When I was a kid I just used to watch Oldham,' he confessed in an interview with *The Times* ahead of the 2002 World Cup showdown with Brazil. 'They are still my heroes. Andy Ritchie was my hero and I loved the goals he scored.'

It was during this spell that Scholes caught the attention of the scouts at Oldham, providing the perfect platform to follow in the footsteps of Ritchie and fellow stars such as Frankie Bunn, and he joined their Centre of Excellence. However, Scholes confessed that this period did not bring the best out of him, and, when Manchester United came knocking, there was only one place he wanted to be.

Despite being devoted to Manchester United, Scholes admits there is a small desire to return to the team he supported as a boy.

'I always supported Oldham as a kid, so it might be nice to go and play for them later in my career. But you never know, the club might want to sell me before then. You don't know what the future holds. It might be nice one day, though.'

A move to United was sealed when Brian Kidd was presenting the trophy at a schools football final and it was there he finalised plans to bring the red-headed midfielder to one of the grandest academies in British football. After talking to the school, and Scholes's parents, Kidd followed through on Ferguson's pledge to bring only the best local talent to The Cliff – Manchester United's formidable former training ground.

Scholes admits that the Manchester United youth team of the early 1990s owe much of their success to Kidd. He said, 'Brian Kidd was the main reason for getting all the lads who've gone on to win trophies. He was the main person and we have a lot to thank him for.'

Scholes signed as a trainee on 8 July 1991 and, at these first training sessions with United, he met up with David Beckham, Nicky Butt and the Neville brothers – the players with whom he would dominate the footballing world less than a decade later.

Alex Ferguson, meanwhile, freely admits that the only player he was sure would graduate from the academy was Ryan Giggs, and Paul Scholes certainly had doubts hanging over his head. There were question marks as to whether the diminutive midfielder, who was plagued by bronchitis and growing pains, would stand the rigours of first-team action. There was no doubting Scholes's talent – and his teammates knew not to be fooled by his size – but while the likes of David Beckham, Simon Davies and George Spitzer were playing week in, week out for the youth team, Scholes was not afforded such a regular run. He could not be considered a late bloomer, but his ascent into the team was certainly more guarded than that of Nicky Butt and in particular Giggs, who terrorised First Division defenders from the tender age of 17. Scholes was not a member of the 1992 FA Youth Cup-winning squad, contrary to popular belief, and the midfielder admits there were times he wondered if he would make his first-team debut, due to the nagging doubts over his stature. In a programme looking at the legendary Manchester United youth team, Scholes confessed, 'There is a time you wonder if you are ever going to make it. Thankfully I filled out.' The rest of the footballing world grew to be thankful, as Scholes proved himself never shy when throwing himself into the tackle – however, with varying degrees of success – culminating in his being sent off for the national side against Sweden in 1999, a heated moment that gave him the dubious distinction of being the only England player to be sent off at the old Wembley.

Scholes was gradually blooded into the senior side when players such as Ryan Giggs and David Beckham had cemented a first-team place. Certainly, few pundits have ever been as catastrophically wrong as Alan Hansen, when, at the time Ferguson replaced his old guard with the fresh-faced youngsters who had worked their way up through the ranks at Old Trafford, he said, 'You will never win anything with kids.' In the early 1990s, competition for places in the youth team at The Cliff was great, let alone the Championship-winning first team.

Competing for the four midfield positions in the youth team alone were David Beckham, Ryan Giggs, Keith Gillespie, Robbie Savage and Nicky Butt, as well as Scholes. All these players have been capped by their country and played consistently in the Premier League. Giggs was being used as an auxiliary striker to free up space on the wing, where the Irishman Gillespie could trouble defenders with his sheer pace. Scholes, however, took the chance when it was given to him, scoring the first in a 3–0 win over Blackburn Rovers as United stormed to victory in the Lancashire FA Youth Cup final of 1993. This was the season that Scholes was given a more regular run in the youth team; however, there was to be major disappointment when United were unable to retain the FA Youth Cup. Scholes netted from the penalty spot but was unable to prevent a 4–1 aggregate drubbing at the hands of Leeds United. A crowd of more than 30,000 packed inside Elland Road for the return leg, with United trailing 2–0 from the first game at Old Trafford. The Neville brothers, Beckham, Gillespie and Robby Savage all lined up alongside Scholes in a formidable-looking team, but it was the Yorkshire side who took their chances, and denied United's golden generation the joy of retaining the FA Youth Cup.

Throughout his career Scholes would be known for his late, surging runs into the penalty area, picking up any loose ball to drill home with pinpoint accuracy. It is a trait Ferguson admits he had from a young age.

'He has an awareness of what's happening around him on the edge of the box which is better than most players,' he said. 'As a kid he always had a knack of arriving in the penalty area just at the right time.'

Eric Harrison, the youth team coach credited with the success of United's brilliant youth team, told the *News of the World* that Scholes worried whether his stature would hold him back from the dream life of a professional footballer. 'Paul was full of fear and believed Sir Alex was going to release him because of his size,' he said. 'Paul honestly thought his height would count against him, but he was one of a clutch of tiny tots we had then. I told him stature doesn't matter, that he had the quality to succeed, and he's proved me right. I told him to look at David Beckham, Nicky Butt and Ryan Giggs and it would make him feel better. Becks was only 5ft 3in but unlike Paul he didn't worry too much about his stature, and I think Scholes was comforted by that. I honestly believe that evening was the turning point for Paul. He never looked back but his friendship with his other United mates helped him survive a mental crisis.'

Aside from youth team affairs, 1993 brought international success for Scholes, as he helped England capture the European Under-18 Championship on home soil. United teammates Gary Neville and Chris Casper played their part alongside Sol Campbell and Robbie Fowler, and it was Fowler, then a young

Liverpool striker, who was the hero of the tournament, hitting a hat-trick in the 5–1 demolition of Spain as England's young charges surged to the final. Buoyed on by a crowd of 24,000 at Nottingham Forest's City Ground on 25 July, Scholes – used mostly as a substitute – helped to bring England their first youth silverware for 13 years. Darren Caskey – then of Tottenham Hotspur – struck the telling goal against Turkey in the final, much to the delight of the massive crowd gathered in Nottingham.

Only two days before the final, on 23 January 1993, Scholes had signed as a professional for Manchester United and was now ready for the step-up in class.

II

Alex Ferguson had endured an inauspicious start to life at Old Trafford, going three years without winning a trophy before landing the FA Cup with a victory over Crystal Palace in the 1990 replay. The club had gone a quarter of a century without winning at the top tier of English football and victory at Wembley proved the springboard as United rediscovered their appetite for silverware. In the same year Ferguson led the Red Devils to UEFA Super Cup success over Barcelona and the League Cup a year later in 1992.

Below first-team affairs, the 1993–94 season would prove pivotal for Scholes and the rest of the youngsters eager to prove their worth to Alex Ferguson.

So, as part of natural progression, Scholes and many of the

Manchester United youth team swiftly graduated to the reserves side, where they were to be moulded into first-team regulars by reserve team coach Jimmy Ryan, who had himself narrowly missed out on a place in Manchester United's legendary squad of 1968.

Ryan was known for being a no-nonsense coach who rarely lavished praise despite the wealth of talent that had landed on his doorstep from the youth ranks. However, in an interview with the *Observer* shortly before Scholes made his first-team debut, Ryan dropped his guard, and spoke highly of the young red-headed midfielder.

'He has a football brain,' he said. 'He understands what you are saying, what you want from him and he is able to improvise. All we have done is work on his strength and fitness and help him adjust to the greater thinking speed that is required at higher levels.'

As Scholes was asserting himself at youth and reserve level, the first team began to gel under Ferguson in perhaps the most chaotic time in the domestic game. The foundation of the Premier League in 1992 shook British football to the core as Rupert Murdoch's BSkyB empire changed the face of the English football with lucrative television coverage and the money this generated for the football clubs. To prepare for the first season in the new top-flight league, Ferguson pulled one of his greatest masterstrokes, plucking Eric Cantona from champions Leeds United for £1.2 million in November 1992. Prior to signing the Frenchman, the Reds had struggled in the league. With Brian McClair and Mark Hughes off form and Dion Dublin suffering a broken leg, United had found it hard to score goals – but

Cantona's arrival heralded a change in fortunes for Ferguson. The Scottish tactician had given the side a solid back four in Denis Irwin, Steve Bruce, Gary Pallister and Paul Parker. But now, with Ryan Giggs announcing himself on the world stage, Manchester United marched on to be crowned the first Premier League champions, capped so gloriously by Steve Bruce's two headed goals against Sheffield Wednesday.

Mark Hughes admits he watched Manchester United's youth team with a sense of expectation when it became clear they were destined for the big time.

'I could see as soon as these boys joined they were special,' the Welshman said of the United youngsters. 'Scholes is a great talent; the way he strikes the ball is phenomenal.'

And the success that the first team were beginning to enjoy gave the youth team something to strive for. 'All these young players have watched the success I was part of from afar and seen how the game should be played,' Hughes continued. 'Now they look as though they'll be playing for years to come. You could always see the talent but there was no fear in them – they could play in front of thirty thousand. They can go as far as they want to and will be a fixture in the side.'

The 1993–94 season brought even greater success for the first team as they swept to the double of Premier League and FA Cup, with new signing Roy Keane – one of the club's greatest servants – adding more steel to the midfield. Ferguson had built a team of champions, but, with the careers of midfield general Brian Robson and Brian McClair reaching their twilight, Ferguson knew he would need players who could fight for the Premier

17

League for years to come. January 1994 brought the club to a standstill with the death of Sir Matt Busby, but, with his ideals deeply entrenched at Old Trafford, the club would drive forward to dominate English football.

To underline the strength in depth that Ferguson had installed at Old Trafford, the Reserves won the Pontin's Reserve League in the 1993–94 season as the graduates from the youth side comfortably made the step up to the next level. Scholes was now pushing for a chance to shine in the first team, and, on 21 September 1994, Ferguson duly obliged.

The League Cup had proved the perfect setting for Ferguson to blood his young charges, and Northwest neighbours Port Vale were the unhappy recipients. At the time there were regulations against fielding weakened sides in the competition, but Ferguson put his faith in youth, with Scholes making his debut along with Simon Davies; but by this time David Beckham, Nicky Butt and Gary Neville had already made *their* first-team bows. United came from behind the snatch a 2–1 win at Vale Park.

Ten of the United squad that had battled to victory over Liverpool in the first team's Premier League the weekend before the tie with Port Vale did not make the short trip to Vale Park, as Ferguson cast half an eye over forthcoming Champions League action. Brian McClair, Denis Irwin and Roy Keane were the wise heads brought in to add experience to the young side, but many saw the team put forward by Ferguson as breaching Rule 18 of the Football League, whereby a club must not field a weakened side, with a local MP threatening the Reds with the Trade Descriptions Act.

Judging by the result, few can argue that Ferguson got his tactics – and selection – spot on.

Scholes was delighted to make his first-team bow and enjoyed every minute of his fairytale debut.

'Scoring two goals was a dream come true,' he said. 'To play for the first team at all was brilliant, and then to score two goals was just amazing. There were so many younger players playing, the Gaffer just told us all to go out and enjoy it, and we did!'

Despite the jealous furore the match created, it proved to be a dream debut for Scholes as he bagged both goals to confirm the rumours of a potential superstar emerging from within Old Trafford. Journalists gushed over the match-winning performances, striking comparisons with both Eric Cantona and Mark Hughes as Scholes announced himself on the first-team stage in style.

Another Manchester United trainee, Phil Neville, admits that the patience and planning of the Manchester United coaching staff were the driving force behind their ascent to the first team. 'Everything we do at United prepares you for this,' he said. 'It's done in steps, from youth team to reserve team to first team to internationals.

'The message then was that we had to work hard and we might make it. Brian Kidd used to say we had to improve a little bit every year – if we did we might make it.'

While the boss's defiant stance on youth brought controversy and pressure – particularly from the Football League – these matches were all about laying the foundation for the Ferguson dynasty at Manchester United, and history would dictate that the Scot, as always, was absolutely right. The gulf in class between the new Premier League and all who sit below them was now becoming all too apparent, and a victory between what was essentially Manchester United's reserve side over Port Vale served as an early warning of the friction the Premier League had caused since its inception.

Ferguson's faith in youth may have courted controversy throughout British football, but for Scholes it was a dream debut, and he was now ready to stake a claim for a first-team place at Manchester United Football Club.

Chapter 2

YOU CAN
WIN EVERYTHING
WITH KIDS

'Taking risks is part of football and I will never shy away from this.'
SIR ALEX FERGUSON

Three United stalwarts headed for the Old Trafford exit door in the summer, with Andrei Kanchelskis, Paul Ince and Mark Hughes all moving on to pastures new, causing many to question the wisdom of Sir Alex Ferguson. Alan Hansen claimed, 'You will never win anything with kids' after Ferguson's youngsters succumbed to a 3–1 defeat to Aston Villa on the opening day of the 1995–96 season. Three first-half goals proved too much for the fledgling United heroes, despite David Beckham's fabulous late free kick. Scholes started the game alongside fellow youth team products Nicky Butt and the Neville brothers, while Beckham was a half-time substitute. Scholes picked up his one and only booking of the season at Villa Park but Ferguson kept faith in the young attacker, who started the next league match against West Ham as United picked up their first points of the season. Scholes repaid his manager with the opening goal shortly after the interval to edge United ahead against the east Londoners. A Steve Bruce own goal shortly after hauled the Hammers back into contention, but the home side were not to be denied – and Roy Keane netted the winner on 67 minutes. United continued to pick up the points with Scholes in the side, although the usually sturdy partnership of Bruce and Pallister at the heart of the defence failed to keep a clean sheet during nervy victories over Wimbledon, Blackburn and Everton. Scholes showed his increasing value to Ferguson's new side with goals in both halves to fire United to a 3–0 victory over hapless Bolton Wanderers at Old Trafford in mid-September. Bobby Charlton, perhaps the most famous of the Busby Babes, admitted he was almost brought to tears by the breathtaking beauty of United's new, young side. 'I felt emotional, as did a few people around me in the stand,' he is quoted in the *Daily Mail* as saying. 'When you have seen young players like these grow up you hope they will all do well. The kids are accustomed to playing together from the youth side. They are getting bigger, stronger and more experienced. They love passing the ball and playing good football. To see it all come together in a first team game was fantastic. People were worrying before the match about having six lads under 21 playing but I thought it would not be a problem,' he continued.

'You can't plan something like this, but we are lucky all these lads came together at the same time – there is more in the pipeline too. There is something for people here to look forward to for a long, long time. Apart from Ryan Giggs, they are all English. I am sure one day they can go on and play for their country and they will do England proud.'

Manchester United's youngsters had proved they could handle life at the highest level and began to dominate domestic affairs, buoyed by the imminent return of Eric Cantona. United were held to successive draws by Sheffield Wednesday and Liverpool, where Cantona announced his return to the side with a 71st-minute penalty to rescue a point against the Merseysiders. October brought a handful of high-octane derbies to whet the appetite of United fans, and Scholes bagged the only goal against rivals Manchester City to give the red half of the city the bragging rights until the Maine Road rematch. Andy Cole, a £7 million signing from Newcastle, had begun to establish himself in the side and provided another attacking option to the mercurial Eric Cantona. Scholes was replaced by Lee Sharpe on the hour mark, but the damage had already been done, and United's youngsters could celebrate their first derby victory.

Scholes then netted another brace in the next league fixture against Chelsea, who had nabbed United stalwart Mark Hughes in the summer. The Oldham-born youngster was seen as the natural successor to the combative Welshman, and his two goals at Stamford Bridge proved Ferguson was right to place his faith in kids. While Andy Cole may not have been bursting the net, a four-goal haul against Chelsea ensured Ferguson would lose little sleep over his new acquisition. The return of Cantona, the talismanic Frenchman, threatened Scholes's place in the starting line-up the most, given the hefty sum paid for England international Andy Cole. However, Ferguson admitted the form of Scholes meant it was impossible to leave him out of the side. 'I couldn't leave Paul out,' he told the *Mail on Sunday* after the win over Chelsea. 'He is a smashing player and his goal ratio is now 16 in 21 league games.'

However, a trip to battle-hardened Arsenal with seasoned veterans Steve Bould, Tony Adams and David Platt proved a bridge too far for the young United side, who fell to a 14th-minute strike from Dutchman Dennis Bergkamp. Unfazed by the setback, Scholes returned to goalscoring form at the first opportunity as United swept aside Southampton with a 4–1 win at Old Trafford. A Ryan Giggs brace and one from Scholes put United three goals to the good inside ten minutes, while Andy Cole netted in the second half before Neil Shipperley's late consolation. United suffered a dip in form and Scholes would not taste victory in a red shirt until the New Year, as he dropped out of the side at the end of 1995 through illness and a dip in form.

Disappointing defeats to rivals Leeds and Liverpool sparked a barren run for the Reds, who drew with Chelsea, Sheffield Wednesday and Aston Villa to lose ground on the Premier League pacesetters. Ferguson admitted that taking risks is a massive part of football and had no regrets in blooding his young charges. 'As soon as the youngsters began to come through I had to give them a chance,' he told the *Daily Record*.

'My back four – Neville, Bruce, Pallister, Irwin – and goalie Schmeichel are the best in England. It is a solid foundation with Cantona and Cole back after suspension and injury and I also knew if Ryan Giggs was fit I would have the very best front men. The game was in midfield,' he continued. 'After losing Kanchelskis and Ince would Beckham, Butt and Scholes be able to handle it? I put great store on the influence of Roy Keane, who is a marvellous player, although he has been sent off twice. Taking risks is part of football and I will never shy away from this.'

Scholes saw his first action of 1996 in the goalless draw with the Villains but had to wait until February to taste success, with Lee Sharpe's solitary goal giving United all three points against Blackburn Rovers at Old Trafford. Newcastle United's seemingly insurmountable lead at the top of the Premier League was slowly being whittled down by a battling and resilient Manchester United side, who closed the gap to just four points with a six-goal thumping of Bolton Wanderers. United were already three goals to the good when Scholes replaced Eric Cantona with 20 minutes remaining, but he soon made his mark on the contest, finding the back of the net within five minutes. He swiftly bagged a second on 79 minutes before Nicky Butt's last-gasp effort. Another former youth team hero, David Beckham, had started the rout in the fifth minute and Ferguson could barely contain his delight at the success of his young charges.

'We thought they were certainties,' he said of the youth team of 1992. 'Absolutely no doubts that they would make first-team players. It goes in cycles. I can go back to my school football and that's what I remember. Suddenly, one school or one area would have a great group of players and, with clubs, you would notice it was the ones that worked hard with their youth teams. We have already worked particularly hard at it here,' he continued in the *Guardian*. 'That particular youth team of the early Nineties represented a high point in terms of intensity. We managed to get a group of players from different parts of the country, and they became a team.'

Club captain Steve Bruce echoed his boss's sentiments, hoping that Newcastle – his home town club – could base their success around homegrown talent also. 'The boss has always produced young players but this has been a tremendous success,' he told the *Northern Echo*. 'Paul Scholes is our leading scorer and Phil Neville has been impressive. It is a lesson for others, if a club of our stature and size can do it, anybody can.'

Kevin Keegan had spent close to £40 million on bringing a cosmopolitan flair to Newcastle United, with the likes of David Ginola and Faustino Asprilla producing moments of genius and exasperation in equal measure. While Scholes's ascent to the first team may have been blocked by the £7 million signing Andy Cole and the mercurial Eric Cantona, Ferguson admitted he was delighted to have such a capable player to come off the bench and change the course of any game. Scholes had netted 13 goals from his 16 starts and, despite asthma-related problems, remained key to Alex Ferguson's plans. Out of the many youth team players who had made the first team this season, Scholes was arguably the outstanding performer, yet could not guarantee a starting place in the side.

'He is an ideal player to have on the bench,' Ferguson told the *People*. 'It is tragic for him being kept out but his time will come. Some find it hard to get into a game when they are sent on but

Paul can pick up the pace of the game immediately. It is a vital stage of the season coming up and I may have to rest one of the strikers and Paul will get his chance.'

United worked tirelessly to overcome Newcastle at the top of the Premier League, and Scholes played an active role in victories over Arsenal, Coventry and Leeds. The goals, meanwhile, had dried up and a defeat to Southampton at the Dell, coupled with a 1–1 draw with Queens Park Rangers, ensured a nail-biting end to the league season. Scholes did not take part in the victory over Newcastle at St James' Park that marked the turning point in their season. Eric Cantona scored against the run of play to send United back to Old Trafford with all three points, much to the frustration of Magpies boss Kevin Keegan, who had already lost his cool in a television interview, irked by Alex Ferguson's mind games. Scholes started his first game for nearly five months at the end of April and led United to a 5–0 demolition of Nottingham Forrest. Ferguson had lost patience in Andy Cole, who had yet to find his best form in a red shirt, and Scholes repaid his manager's faith with a goal just before half time that set United on their way. 'I thought that, if we were going to get a result and score, then Scholes had to be given his opportunity, because we know he is a marvellous scorer,' Ferguson explained. 'We knew he would be fresh and had the crowd behind him and that they would not get anxious if he missed chances. If he was going to play, it had to be upfront from the start. Once we decided that, Andy had to be the one to step down. It was not an easy decision but it was the right one.'

The title now seemed destined for Old Trafford, with United

recovering a 12-point deficit on their Northeast rivals, vindicating Ferguson's decision to trust in his young players. A 3-0 victory over Middlesbrough at the Riverside Stadium concluded a breathtaking finale to league affairs, with Steve Bruce holding the trophy aloft in front of the travelling United faithful. While Eric Cantona may have grabbed the headlines with a succession of crucial goals, goalkeeper Peter Schmeichel had been frustrating opposition attackers, allowing United to squeeze through on a succession of one-goal victories. However, the giant Dane, signed from Brøndby for £500,000, believed the club owed a large debt to the young players – as he summed up the season. 'These youngsters have come into the side and delivered in every game,' he is quoted as telling the *Daily Mail*. 'We had a bad December but the way they come through and the way the team is playing now makes me feel really sorry that I am getting old. I am 33 this year and time is running out for me but I would love to have played with these kids for the next 10 or 15 years. They will just go on and on.

'People call these outstanding young stars kids. In a way I do that myself. But believe me, in footballing terms they are not kids any more. They deserve to be recognised as senior footballers with Manchester United. They are adult players who possess great ability and they have proved they have the bottle to play in vital games with the championship trophy on the horizon. They are gaining great experience but they can still go out there and enjoy their football.

'They don't feel any press, that is the tremendous thing they have about them. From the age of 13 or 14 they have been brought up properly here. They have learned the attitude of the club, the way to conduct themselves and the ways of a United footballer. They possess great discipline and to see them developing the way they have done has been stunning.'

Schmeichel also confessed that United's elder statesmen had been rejuvenated by the current crop of youngsters: 'The senior players can't stop enjoying playing alongside these exciting kids,' he said. 'Sometimes I just stand in my penalty area smiling about the way the youngsters can play. It's fantastic to watch them. Unbelievable. They just keep delivering, and that's why I would love to go on in this team with these boys.'

With the Premier League trophy safely locked away at Old Trafford, United turned their attention to the FA Cup, where they would contest the eagerly anticipated final with Liverpool at Wembley. Lee Sharpe, who had set Old Trafford alight with some wonderful performances despite his tender years, admitted that the desire of Scholes and his fellow young stars was the driving force behind the club's success.

'They want success and they want it now,' he told the *People*. 'Their desire is just awesome. People say you do not appreciate winning until you get older and you realise how hard it is. But the lads like the Nevilles, David Beckham, Nicky Butt and Paul Scholes have a real appetite for success and they want to grab it while they can. Whether or not we are lucky enough to do the double this year, this team can go on winning things for years to come. It is just the start for them.'

Sharpe said Ferguson's blueprint for success was beginning to pay dividends at the club. 'The manager has put the foundations in place and he has assembled a squad of players just made for winning', he said. 'Take the young lads, they have been schooled for the big time ever since they joined the club. Whether you are in the A team or the first team the opposition treat every game against Manchester United as a cup final. The players have to handle that from day one at this club.

'Although playing in the first team is a bigger stage and there is more at stake, the philosophy is exactly the same at junior level. That is why the youngsters have just slotted in. Everyone knows what is expected of them.'

Scholes started on the bench at Wembley as Ferguson opted for Cole's experience to lead the line alongside Eric Cantona. However, a lacklustre first half saw Scholes enter the fray shortly after the hour mark. The final was won five minutes from time, when Cantona took advantage of chaos in the Liverpool penalty area to guide the ball home from 18 yards.

Over the summer United looked to build on their success by snaring Blackburn's prolific frontman Alan Shearer in a big-money deal. Rovers, meanwhile, were reported to want Paul Scholes in exchange for the Newcastle-born striker. The Oldham-born attacker was, despite his excellent form, not a first-team regular at Old Trafford, but Scholes quickly moved to quell the speculation.

'I have no intention of going anywhere', he is quoted in the *Daily Mirror* as saying. 'As far as I am concerned, I am contracted to United for the next three years. Exciting things are happening at Old Trafford and I want to be a part of it.'

Transfer speculation was rife throughout the summer, as England played host to the European Championships, bringing the Continent's finest players to the British Isles. United moved quickly to snap up Czech midfielder Karel Poborsky, who played an important role in firing his nation to the finals, where they were narrowly beaten by Germany at Wembley Stadium. Also joining the Old Trafford ranks were Dutch goalkeeper Raimond Van der Gouw, defender Ronnie Johnson and Jordi Cruyff, son of the legendary Johan. Perhaps Ferguson's best piece of summer wheeler-dealing came in the form of unknown Norwegian striker Ole Gunnar Solskjaer, who cost £1.5 million from FC Molde. Ferguson had missed out on Alan Shearer, who had helped fire England to the semi-finals of Euro '96 before opting to join home-town club Newcastle United for £15 million. Ferguson's new-look squad headed off on a pre-season tour of Northern Ireland as the new boys looked to impress the boss ahead of the Charity Shield curtain raiser at Wembley. Scholes announced his intentions for an automatic-starting berth with a first-half hat-trick against Portadown, who were blown away by the slick Reds in a comfortable 5–0 win. United also contested the Umbro Cup back in England, but lost 2–1 to Ajax in a fiery encounter at Nottingham Forrest's City Ground. Scholes came to blows with Dutch defender Danny Blind in a penalty-box fracas, but neither player received his marching orders from the referee.

Scholes was handed a starting place in the Charity Shield against Newcastle, which United won at a canter with a 4–0 drubbing of Keegan's side. Jordi Cruyff took Scholes's place as a substitute as the gulf in class between the two sides looked to have increased over the summer. For the opening encounter of the season, a home game against Everton, Scholes dropped to the bench as Poborsky and Cruyff got their first taste of Premier League action. The match ended in a disappointing 2–2 draw, but Scholes was recalled to the side for the trip to Wimbledon, which the Reds took 3–0 – capped by David Beckham's astonishing goal from the halfway line.

Scholes signed a new contract in September that would tie him to the club until 2001 and returned to the starting line-up at the end of September for a comfortable 2–0 win over Tottenham at Old Trafford. The four-goal drubbing of Newcastle in the Charity Shield counted for little in the first league meeting between the league's top two, who met at St James' Park on 20 October. Scholes replaced Karel Poborsky on 66 minutes with United already shell-shocked and three goals down. He could not help stem the Geordie tide, as Alan Shearer and Philippe Albert scored late on to cap a 5–0 victory for the jubilant Magpies.

Scholes bagged his first goal of the season in a League Cup tie against Swindon at Old Trafford on 23 October. He led the line in a side offering few first-team regulars – and netted what proved to be the winning goal in the 72nd minute.

Scholes kept his starting place for the trip to Southampton three days later with United looking to avenge their 5–0 league drubbing at the hands of Newcastle. Decked out in their now infamous grey strip, United took to the field at The Dell expecting a comfortable trip to the south coast. However, Roy Keane's 21st-minute departure sparked a remarkable nine-goal afternoon, with United losing out 6–3. Scholes scored a consolation in the final minute but an Egil Østenstad hat-trick had already put the result beyond doubt.

The matches were now coming thick and fast for Scholes, who came off the bench in the midweek Champions League game at home to Turkish side Fenerbahce. Ferguson's side were defending their 56-match, 40-year unbeaten record at Old Trafford in European football, which had stood since the Busby era, but a 79th-minute strike from Croat Elvir Bolić destroyed United's proud record. With United reeling from the defeat, west London side Chelsea took full advantage, claiming a 2–1 victory at Old Trafford to continue the disastrous run of form.

Scholes did not see league action until the end of November but could not inspire his side to victory over Middlesbrough, who claimed a 2–2 home draw before seeing their League Cup challenge hit the buffers at Leicester. United were suffering from a crisis of confidence going into the busy Christmas period and were indebted to Scholes for salvaging a point against Sheffield Wednesday on 18 December.Ferguson's side had their odds of retaining the title lengthened to 4–1 and had endured the worst away form of any side in the top half of the table. United had slipped to sixth place in the league, but any talk of their title challenge ending was quickly dispelled as they returned to form with a 5–0 win over Sunderland three days later. Scholes, Cantona and Solskjaer formed a potent strike force, with the Norwegian and Frenchman each bagging a brace to secure a morale-boosting win.

The festive period continued in a similar vein as they thrashed Nottingham Forest 4–0 at the City Ground. Solskjaer, nicknamed the baby-faced assassin, was once again among the goals as United shrugged off their month-long slump. United made it three wins out of three with victory over Leeds before playing out a New Year's Day stalemate with Aston Villa.

United began their defence of the FA Cup days later with a potentially tricky tie against Spurs. Scholes broke the deadlock early in the second half before David Beckham made the points safe. Scholes took his place in the side seven days later for a rematch against the north Londoners, and United's surge up the table gathered pace with a 2–1 victory at White Hart Lane before a comfortable away win at lowly Coventry City.

Scholes continued his run of goals in the FA Cup with an 89th-minute goal against Wimbledon. However, there was to be a late drama, as Robbie Earle equalised in stoppage time to send the tie to an Old Trafford replay. The sides would meet four days later in a league encounter and United continued to struggle, but came from behind to snatch a 2–1 victory.

Scholes's increasing importance to the United side was highlighted before the match, when Ferguson confirmed he would replace Eric Cantona during his two-match ban. 'He has been superb for us,' the Scot told the *Daily Mirror*. 'He has done a great job and will definitely play against Wimbledon. And when Cantona is suspended for a couple of games next month, we could well put him in Eric's role.'

Scholes could not make the most of this opportunity, however, and was forced to endure a two-month layoff from the first team due to a cartilage operation. United had powered their way to the quarter-finals of the Champions League and

Portuguese champions Porto represented a stern test for the United youngsters.

Towards the end of February, Scholes was making a good recovery from his knee operation and Ferguson was relieved to have the 22-year-old back in contention. 'He is about a week in front [of schedule] at the moment and he could even be back playing for the second leg,' he told the *Guardian*. 'That is a heck of a task for the lad, and he will have to get a game under his belt beforehand, but he could come into consideration for that game.'

Scholes returned to league action on 15 March and helped United to a comfortable home win over Sheffield Wednesday, earning a place in the squad for the second leg of the Champions League match with Porto. United had won the first leg 4–1, capped by a rare goal from centre-back David May. A thoroughly professional away performance saw United progress with a goalless draw in Portugal. Scholes replaced Ole Solskjaer on 71 minutes.

Scholes returned to first-team action in early April, but was still not afforded a starting place, settling for a late cameo in the disastrous 3–2 defeat to Derby that slowed United's charge towards the title. Domestic affairs were put on the backburner as United looked to reach their first Champions League final under Ferguson. The Scot had made no secret of his desire to succeed in Europe – a feat that would put him alongside the great Matt Busby – but standing in their way were a powerful, organised Borussia Dortmund side, on the crest of a wave after a magnificent season. Scholes again came off the bench in the final ten minutes but could not inspire an equaliser, with René Tretschok's 76th-minute goal giving the Germans a healthy lead to take to Old Trafford.

Three days later, Scholes was finally given a starting berth, as United travelled to Lancashire neighbours Blackburn looking to continue their good league form. Ferguson was delighted as his attacking trio of Scholes, Cantona and Cole all found the back of the net in a pulsating encounter at Ewood Park. Cantona and Scholes had put United 3–1 ahead and, despite a late Paul Warhurst effort, United were able to cling on for three priceless points. Ferguson kept faith with the 22-year-old for the crucial derby match against Liverpool and was not to be disappointed, as United took a massive step towards retaining the league title with victory over Liverpool.

A collector's-item brace from Gary Pallister heaped more woe on Liverpool keeper David James, who had a torrid time dealing with United's set pieces, contributing to a 3–1 win for the visitors.

United were gathering pace at a crucial point in the season and Ferguson said they were confident of Champions League victory on home soil: 'I can accept some people writing us off', he said in the *Daily Mirror*. 'I understand that to a certain degree because the Germans are a good side, but we are capable of beating them. They might think they are through but any time thinking that with us usually gets a fright. I think the players are hitting form at just the right time of the season; they are all very upbeat and ready to go. Dortmund are a good team but if we go about the job in the right way we will be OK.'

Ferguson claimed that his young side's potential was limitless and they were in charge of their own destiny. 'There is no saying what level this team can get to,' he continued. 'We are young and have to keep proving ourselves. We have improved with each game in the Champions League and Wednesday could be the night that will make a lot of our players. I have so many tremendous options. Paul Scholes is playing well. Then there is Eric Cantona, Nicky Butt, Cole and Solskjaer. We have ammunition there.' Unfortunately for Ferguson, Dortmund proved too strong and too tactically astute for the young side – and Lars Ricken's solitary goal dumped United out at the semi-final stage. While European glory was out of reach for another season, United had proved their mettle and Ferguson had vowed that they would keep improving year on year.

However, there was still a second league title to be won, and Scholes played four games in eight days for United, who retained their title despite being held to three draws in those final matches. After a 26-year wait for a league title, Ferguson had delivered Manchester United four in five years, and was confident his young side could go on and dominate English football for the rest of the decade and beyond.

Paul Scholes could now look forward to a more prolonged spell in the United first team – especially after bursting onto the international scene for England in Le Tournoi, staged in France. However, the rest of Manchester was plunged into mourning as Eric Cantona announced his retirement, ending his five-year reign as King of Old Trafford.

Scholes told the *Mirror* he was prepared to step out from the shadow of Cantona, and try to fill the void left by his departure. 'I am very determined about my career and I desperately want to be a part of Manchester United,' he said. 'I am not one for saying I am going to do this and that but my aim is to be playing here in ten years' time.

'It has been pretty flattering to be mentioned in the same breath as Eric but I am happy with what I have achieved at my age. The manager always told me to be patient because in the long run I will play plenty of games for United.'

Ferguson, meanwhile, was not prepared to settle for domestic dominance alone, and he set his sights on European glory, admitting that his disappointment at Euro failings had all but cancelled out his joy at league success. 'The only cloud on the season was out failure to go all the way in the European Champions League,' he told the *Mirror*. 'Losing both semi-final ties 1–0 against Dortmund after we dominated much of both games without being able to score left me quite devastated and I am sure our supporters shared that emotion.

'But I'm thinking positively again. Reaching the last four was an indication of the progress this team has made in Europe and proved we can handle the twin challenges of competing at home and abroad in the same season. The improvements we showed over the campaign also pleased me. I believe we are very close now to winning the ultimate European trophy. We need to take just one more step and then we would have an outstanding chance.'

United opened the season against FA Cup winners Chelsea in the Charity Shield, with new signing Teddy Sheringham partnering Andy Cole in attack, while Scholes fell back to central midfield alongside Nicky Butt. David Beckham's meteoric rise to superstardom began to have an effect on his life at Old Trafford and Ferguson sensationally dropped the midfielder for the season's curtain raiser at Wembley.

'My original plan to rest both Beckham and Gary Neville was correct, without question,' he said in the build-up to the game. 'You have to take a long-term view with young players. They understand that and know how concerned I was about their playing for England in France. In midfield we are very fortunate to have so many good players at the club. In Paul Scholes, Nicky Butt and Roy Keane, I have a tremendous midfield three.'

United won the match 4–2 on penalties after a 1–1 draw in normal time. With just days until the start of a Cantona-less season, Ferguson said that the club would survive despite the loss of Cantona, thanks to Scholes and his fellow youth team graduates.

'There was a numbness about the place,' he told the *Sunday Mirror*. 'Now, we have personalities like Paul Scholes, Roy Keane and David Beckham. Thereby the transition of the team has overshadowed Eric – which is not an easy thing to do. Supporters can't dwell on the loss any more than the players can. They are Manchester United fans. They will always support the team in red.'

United's Premier League rivals Arsenal, Newcastle and Chelsea all spent big in the summer months, acquiring foreign imports in the hope of dislodging the champions. United began the defence of their title in north London at White Hart Lane against Teddy Sheringham's former employers. Jeered every time he touched the ball, United's new acquisition endured a torrid start to life in red, missing an open goal and a penalty. However, two goals in the last ten minutes saw United get their season off to a winning start.

Alex Ferguson had an embarrassment of riches in the attacking third, with Scholes and Jordi Cruyff playing off frontman Teddy Sheringham in a fluid formation that would keep the Spurs defence guessing for much of the game. United made it two wins out of two with a 1–0 win over Southampton at Old Trafford, but were forced to endure a frustrating evening before David Beckham struck in the 78th minute. Scholes played a more attacking role in the midfield, which was well anchored by Nicky Butt and Roy Keane, but the home side found it tough going against the south coast club, who had set out their stall to play for a draw at the Theatre of Dreams.

Scholes and Sheringham both rattled the woodwork in United's next league fixture – against Leicester – but were forced to settle for a point at Filbert Street as they surrendered their 100 per cent start to the season. Ferguson's keen eye had seen Scholes moved back to a place in midfield, despite playing as a second striker for much of his career. However, with goals hard to come by due to injuries to the United frontmen, Scholes was challenged by Ferguson to start hitting the back of the net.

'We know Scholes can pass the ball and use it well', he told the *Mirror*. 'He is the most imaginative player we have at the club but it is now just a question of getting the right balance. We have a better choice than ever in midfield. You have to go back to the days of Remi Moses, Bryan Robson, Gordon Strachan, Jesper Olsen and Norman Whiteside, who were all very good players.

'But I think what you are going to see with this group is that they will all mature together. They have a far better appearance record than some of those players. The current lot are different and in Scholes I have someone who can play as a striker too. I think, though, his best position is just forward of midfield. It's easy to forget that he came here at 13 and that he has been around for more than 10 years.

'He was unlucky last year when he picked up a knee injury but it was a big bonus for the boy to get his first England cap in the summer but I think it had been coming for a while.' Teddy Sheringham answered his manager's call for more goals, as he netted his first in United colours in a 2–0 win over Everton as United kept pace with Chelsea and Arsenal. The comfortable victory at a difficult ground such as Goodison Park sent out a message to United's title rivals, and Ferguson said consistency in selection had been they key to their success.

'I don't care whether we are awesome or not,' he is quoted as saying in the *Mirror*. 'What I do know is that this present side has been together for a couple of years now and there has not been that many changes. They are gathering physical strength as well as authority in games, which young players eventually get. We hope they will maintain that. We also know that you have to have a great hunger to win trophies and I think that is important to them.

'In a lot of cases the players are born with that natural hunger

– others develop it. But we have been lucky over the last six years as players have thrived on success. We have also been lucky that certain individuals are born winners. Bryan Robson, Steve Bruce and Brian McClair. They have made quite an impact and have been followed by players like Roy Keane, the Nevilles, David Beckham and Paul Scholes, who are all winners with a great desire.'

Scholes took leave of the United first team at the end of August due to the return of Andy Cole, who started alongside Teddy Sheringham in attack. Scholes returned on 13 September, as United welcomed West Ham to Old Trafford, and bagged his first goal of the season, a goal that proved to be the winner in the 76th minute as United battled to a 2–1 victory. Ferguson had referred to Scholes as his 'little nuisance' on more than one occasion, due to his ability to cause a selection headache for his boss, and continued the trend against the Hammers.

The goal was enough to earn Scholes a starting place in United's first Champions League outing, which pitted them against FC Košice, who became the first ever Slovakian club to reach the group stages of the Champions League. After reaching the latter stages of the competition the previous season, there was now a furore surrounding Manchester United and the Champions League, with many believing it was their destiny to reclaim the trophy.

United legend George Best, perhaps the key protagonist in their only previous success in the competition, told the *Daily Record* that United's current crop must write their own history. 'United will only be judged when they have done what we did,' he said. 'They have done it domestically and now they have to repeat that success in Europe. We did it, and when you go to Old Trafford and see Bobby Charlton, Nobby Stiles, Paddy Crerand, Alex Stepney and Billy Foulkes you realise that is the bottom line. Ryan Giggs is one of the main men now. And David Beckham is verging on being great.

'United also have three or four other players in their early twenties in Nicky Butt, Paul Scholes and the Neville brothers. They were unlucky last year because I don't think people realised just what a good side Borussia Dortmund were. This time it is going to be even tougher.'

Alongside the Slovakian minnows, United were drawn against Turin giants Juventus and Dutch side Feyenoord. United brushed aside Košice with a 3–0 victory, knowing there would be sterner tests on their way to possible Champions League glory. A disappointing goalless draw with Bolton followed before the first of many epic clashes with title hopefuls.

Ruud Gullit's Chelsea presented the first real test of the season for Manchester United and took the lead on 25 through a Henning Berg own-goal. Scholes bagged his second goal of the season to restore parity before former Red Mark Hughes reclaimed Chelsea's advantage. Ole Gunnar Solskjaer struck in the dying minutes to snatch a point for Ferguson's side. The stalemate served only Arsenal, however, who moved clear at the top of the table. United then lost further ground with a disastrous defeat to Leeds United on 27 September, which was far from ideal preparation for the visit of Juventus four days later.

The match proved to be a cracker. Juve took the lead in the

first minute through Alessandro Del Piero, only for Sheringham, Scholes and Giggs to fire United two goals ahead. Frenchman Zinédine Zidane struck a last-minute goal in vain for the visitors, who could not overturn a 3–2 deficit as the night belonged to the home side.

Journalists gushed over Manchester United's performance, which was full of resilience and guile, with David Beckham admitting that the young side had learned from the mistakes of the previous year.

'We were shell-shocked to say the least to concede that goal after 20 seconds,' Beckham told the *Mirror*. 'But it is one of the great Manchester United performances that I have played in. We got the result we wanted. It is all about experience and we learned our lessons of last year.'

Buoyed by their European success, United breezed past Crystal Palace by two goals to nil before being held to a disappointing 2–2 draw with Derby. Scholes netted the opener for United in their next Champions League game at home to Feyenoord. He found the net on the half-hour mark before a Denis Irwin penalty doubled the advantage. Feyenoord hit back in the 83rd minute but could not overturn the deficit, giving United nine points from their first three games in Europe.

Ferguson admitted after the game that he had begun to feel jittery, as his young side needed to learn to kill the game off sooner. 'We tend to do that at times,' he told the *Daily Record*. 'Let teams back into it when we should be killing them off. But at this level you are always going to have to sweat for a bit and it happened to us.'

Following his Champions League opener Johan Cruyff, a Dutch

master and father of injured United player Jordi, told *The Times* that Paul Scholes could etch his name in the history books as one of England's finest. 'People say England has not produced a striker like Paul Scholes before,' Cruyff said. 'But when you look back at Kevin Keegan and how he played with John Toshack, I can see Scholes doing exactly the same role here. Keegan is an example of the kind of player Scholes will become. He has got good vision and an eye for goal. He sees things very early in a game and he showed us that.'

United dispelled any fears of a European hangover with an astonishing win over Barnsley at Old Trafford just days later. Andy Cole hit back at his critics by bagging a hat-trick, while Giggs, Poborsky and Scholes all found the back of the net in a 7–0 victory over the Yorkshire side.

United were in sumptuous form going into November and, with Scholes in the side, continued their free-scoring form with a 6–1 demolition of Sheffield Wednesday. With a place in the last eight of the Champions League all but guaranteed, United stalwart Gary Pallister admitted that he was not surprised at how Fergie's Fledglings had taken domestic and European football by storm. 'It was tantalisingly close for us last year,' he told the *Advertiser*. 'We felt we were the better team against Borussia Dortmund and they went on to win it.'

Regarding United's former youth team charges, Pallister was full of praise. 'I remember when they were all in the youth team,' he said. 'The potential was there, but you always wonder if they will be able to take it on to the bigger stage. But we have all seen them do that, the form they have been producing has been fantastic and the question now is just how much further they can go. I don't think they have reached anything near their potential yet.'

United continued their domestic dominance into the New Year and enjoyed an 11-point lead at the top of the league on 1 March. However, Arsenal had three games in hand and were not going to go down without a fight. A disappointing series of draws and defeats saw United gradually surrender their advantage at the summit of the league, with Arsenal fighting back to claim their first league title since 1991.

Chapter 3

CHAMPIONS
OF EUROPE

It was a sickening thought when I realised I was going to
miss the match in the Nou Camp. The final represented the
biggest game of my life ...'
PAUL SCHOLES

P aul Scholes had announced himself on the world stage in
style with a positive showing in France, but attention now
returned to domestic issues – and the task of regaining the title
from champions Arsenal in what would prove to be the most
remarkable season in Manchester United's history.

Over the summer England boss Glenn Hoddle controversy
when it became clear he had given the squad injections aimed
at boosting vitamin and mineral levels ahead of the crucial
encounters with Colombia and Argentina. Scholes, David
Beckham and Gary Neville were the players involved in the
matches, and Alex Ferguson was left fuming that he had not
been consulted beforehand. However, Neville admitted to the
Journal after the World Cup that there was no shroud of secrecy

over the supplements, and moved to quell the argument, saying that he believed they would become increasingly commonplace in the game.

'There was never any cause for alarm' he said. 'The Germans, Brazilians and Italians have been doing it for 20 years. We're behind on these things but we are willing to listen to new techniques.'

Despite Neville's attempt to cool the row between club and country, the measures taken by the national team had incensed Ferguson, but, with Scholes back and focused on domestic affairs, the rift was soon healed.

The treble-winning season cast legendary status on the Manchester United side and Scholes proved himself as one of the world's best midfielders with crucial goals, assists and dominant performances to help propel the club to unprecedented heights. But it was recognised that the Reds needed a larger squad if they were to mount an assault on three fronts and chief executive Martin Edwards duly obliged, bringing in Swedish winger Jesper Blomqvist to ease the pressure on David Beckham and Ryan Giggs in the wide positions.

The defence was also bolstered with the considerable presence of Jaap Stam, signed for over £10 million from Ajax, while Dwight Yorke became the club's record signing following his move from Aston Villa. The United board had spent over £27 million on new players to avoid the late capitulation endured by the Reds last season, and particularly the disastrous home defeat to Arsenal that all but guaranteed the Gunners the title.

It was to be a massive season for Scholes, who was asked to

fill the considerable boots of Eric Cantona in attack by Alex Ferguson – and he certainly delivered, proving the perfect foil for Roy Keane in a dynamic and dangerous Manchester United midfield. The void left by King Eric the previous season forced changes on Ferguson, and United took time to adjust, contributing to a disjointed campaign that left them trophy-less. But, going into the 1998–99 season, the United squad had never looked in better shape with a solid midfield and four strikers of the quality of Sheringham, Solskjaer, Cole and now Dwight Yorke. Ferguson finally had a squad capable of challenging for all the major trophies in domestic and European football.

The summer had been dominated by takeover talk at Old Trafford, with the press convinced that media mogul Rupert Murdoch would soon take control of the club, a move desperately opposed by the fans, who believed the Australian would suck the soul out of Manchester United for his own gain. There was a fear among supporters that the patient nurturing of the academy system – which was the very foundation of the Busby and Ferguson dynasties – would not be fulfilled by Murdoch, who could bring in cut-price foreign mercenaries in a quick-fix option.

However, come August all talk returned to the pitch, where Ferguson's Reds met Arsenal in the Charity Shield at Wembley. It was not the baptism of fire many had hoped, as Arsène Wenger's side strolled to a 3–0 victory with two goals from Marc Overmars, Christopher Wreh and Nicolas Anelka. Scholes was given a starting place off Andy Cole in attack, but a lethargic performance saw him replaced by Teddy Sheringham with 20 minutes remaining as Arsenal started the new campaign the way they had finished the last: picking up silverware in the sunshine underneath the Twin Towers.

United's runners-up spot in the Premiership meant they had to go through qualification for the Champions League, which pitted them against Polish side LKS Lodz just days after defeat in the season's curtain raiser. Knowing the importance of victory in the home leg, Ferguson put Scholes in the thick of the action, despite a draining World Cup, and the move paid dividends, as he set up Ryan Giggs to give Manchester United an early lead at Old Trafford. A second goal from Andy Cole at the Theatre of Dreams proved too much for Lodz and a stalemate in Poland a fortnight later confirmed United's place in the draw for the group stages of the competition.

League affairs started with the visit of Leicester City to Old Trafford, and it gave Ferguson a chance to blood his new players in front of the home crowd. Scholes played the full ninety minutes as the support striker for Andy Cole. Despite the expectant atmosphere, it took a last-gasp Beckham free kick to salvage a point against the Foxes, as the Reds made an inauspicious start to the campaign.

The disappointing home draw was followed by a stalemate at Upton Park in a game that will not be remembered for the quality of football, but rather for David Beckham enduring the first of many difficult away days following his red card for the Three Lions that marked the capitulation of Glenn Hoddle's men against Argentina. Eager to rest his international stars, Ferguson left Scholes on the bench and, making way for debutant Dwight Yorke, he remained an unused substitute in a drab encounter in east London.

Two draws did not represent the storming resurgence many had expected from Manchester United and Ferguson believed that many of his players were suffering from their summer exertions across the Channel, and Scholes took time to find his form after impressing for England. But United were not off form for long.

Scholes returned to the starting line-up as Manchester United recorded the first of many victories that season with a 4–1 win over Charlton Athletic at Old Trafford. Dwight Yorke grabbed his first goals in United colours, with Ole Gunnar Solskjaer also netting a brace.

Ferguson's embarrassment of riches in the final third were beginning to come good and Scholes was at his industrious best as the Reds recorded consecutive victories for the first time that season with a 2–0 win over Coventry City. The England ace set up Yorke for his third goal in two games, and grabbed another assist as Norwegian defender Ronny Johnson bundled home a second, with United proving too strong for the Sky Blues.

Their reward for victory over LKS Lodz in August was a place in Group D of the Champions League alongside Danish champions Brøndby, European heavyweights Bayern Munich and Barcelona. It was swiftly renamed the Group of Death and represented a difficult challenge even to qualify for the knockout stages of the competition.

The group stages began with the Reds hosting Barcelona in the first of many memorable European nights at Old Trafford that season. Scholes worked tirelessly to stem the tide of the assured and confident Barça midfield and he was on hand to give United a two-goal cushion as he pounced after Barça keeper Ruud Hesp parried Dwight Yorke's audacious overhead kick. But the Catalan club hit back through Sonny Anderson and a Geovani penalty before another wonderful Beckham free kick re-established the hosts' lead.

However, there was to be more drama as Nicky Butt handled in the area, and Luis Enrique rescued a point with the resulting penalty – met with a wall of silence from the stunned crowd. It was a breathless night that would serve as an early warning for the Old Trafford faithful: that European adventures were to be a roller coaster of emotions.

Another 3–0 drubbing at the hands of Arsenal was followed with victory over Liverpool at Old Trafford, as the Ginger Prince took centre stage once again in a stunning man-of-the-match display. United took the lead through a Denis Irwin penalty after Scholes had pressured Jason McAteer into a handball. There was to be no charity with the second, however, as he sent a left-foot rocket inside Brad Friedel's left-hand post to secure a 2–0 win over the Merseysiders.

'It helps erase the memory of the defeat by Arsenal,' Scholes told the *Belfast Times* after the game. 'We played much better after letting ourselves and our fans so badly down against Arsenal.'

Any early-season doubts over Scholes's fitness were soon put to rest as he found the net again, this time at the Olympic

Stadium in Munich, as a powerful, late surge into the box saw him bundle home to give United a 2–1 lead against Bundesliga champions Bayern Munich, in the first of three meetings in the coming months. However, Scholes was again denied match-winning performance, as a late defensive scuffle gifted Ottmar Hitzfeld's side a share of the spoils in Bavaria.

October proved to be a lean month in front of goal for Scholes as Dwight Yorke and Andy Cole established themselves as Ferguson's first-choice strike partnership. The pair began their blossoming partnership with devastating effect as the Reds swept aside Southampton and Wimbledon to remain in touch with early pacesetters Aston Villa. Showing his versatility, Scholes moved back into central midfield alongside Roy Keane to add another goal threat from a deeper position.

United raced to the top of Group D of the Champions League with a 6–2 drubbing of Brøndby in Copenhagen in a game that saw Peter Schmeichel return to his old club.

The club was indebted to Scholes as he came off the bench to rescue a point against Derby County at Pride Park. Striker Deon Burton stunned the travelling supporters by giving the Rams the lead, but with nine minutes remaining Ferguson looked to his bench, with Jordi Cruyff, Jesper Blomqvist and Scholes changing the course of the game late on, Cruyff netting a late equaliser.

'When you bring on players of quality like them, they're all capable of scoring,' said the Scot. 'I only wish Derby had scored earlier because our reaction was terrific.'

Overall, an impressive month was rewarded as the Reds

closed the gap on leaders Aston Villa to one point thanks to a 4–1 win over Everton at Goodison Park. Scholes was at his best as he set up Dwight Yorke for yet another goal for his new side.

November saw the Danish champions travel to Old Trafford in the reverse Champions League fixture, but there was to be no change in fortune as the hosts powered to a 5–0 victory, with Scholes grabbing the fifth. Having burst into the area with another late surge, he rounded two defenders before slotting in to cap another fine home display.

The Old Trafford crowd were forced to endure their one and only stalemate of the season as Newcastle stopped the seemingly relentless charge of Ferguson's side, but they would have hoped for a quieter evening with the visit of Blackburn Rovers to the Theatre of Dreams. Scholes scored either side of a Dwight Yorke goal as United raced to a 3–0 lead, but defensive frailties were brought to light as Roy Hodgson's side stormed back into contention, scoring twice to set up a frantic finish, with the home side limping across the finish line with a 3–2 victory.

Facing a daunting midweek trip to the Nou Camp, United suffered a shock 3–1 defeat to Sheffield Wednesday at Hillsborough, but attention quickly turned to the Champions League duel, which brought another nail-biting evening for Manchester United. Cole and Yorke lit up the Catalan capital but the visitors were to be denied victory by Brazilian superstar Rivaldo, who – playing at the peak of his career – connected with a stunning overhead kick to earn a draw for the hosts.

A point, however, was not enough to see Barcelona through and it was Manchester United and Bayern Munich who progressed from the Group of Death.

Despite playing a massive part in their downfall, Scholes admits Rivaldo is one of the greatest talents he has ever come up against.

'Zidane and Ronaldinho are obviously fantastic players but watching Rivaldo was brilliant,' Scholes confessed to Manchester United's official website. 'He was a different class in the two 3–3 draws.'

The six-goal thriller would be the only time Scholes walked out as a player at Barcelona's giant stadium that season, but late drama would soon come to benefit the Red Devils.

As the domestic season gathered pace United met Yorkshire rivals Leeds, with Scholes once again grabbing an assist as he teed up Roy Keane to fire United in front. However, it took a rare Nicky Butt strike to win the match 3–2 in another high-scoring affair.

In November Brian Kidd left Old Trafford to take over at Blackburn Rovers following Roy Hodgson's departure. It was sad for the players who had risen through the youth ranks to see the man responsible for their ascent to champions leave the club, but the chance for Kidd to make his mark at Ewood Park proved too strong to resist.

With December came a meeting of the Premier League's top two at Villa Park and Scholes gave United a dream start as his drilled effort put the visitors ahead. However, Julian Joachim rescued a point for Villa with a deflected effort that looped cruelly over Peter Schmeichel to maintain their slender advantage at the summit. And the Champions League was put to bed till the New Year with a 1–1 draw with Bayern Munich at Old Trafford. The quarter-final draw pitted Ferguson's Reds against Serie A giants Inter Milan, but first Scholes had to negotiate the physically gruelling Christmas period to help United regain top spot in the league.

However, it was not plain sailing for Ferguson's side, with the first of many fragile performances gifting Tottenham a share of the spoils at White Hart Lane, Scholes's England teammate Sol Campbell the unlikely hero as he netted two late goals to secure a 2–2 draw in north London. This was followed with another draw with Chelsea at Old Trafford before another disastrous home match with Middlesbrough.

Defensive frailties were pounced upon as the Teessiders raced to a three-goal lead. Scholes netted a crucial second to haul his side to within one goal of the visitors, but it proved too much to ask and United tasted home defeat for the first time in the campaign.

But Boxing Day brought a change in fortunes as Scholes, and United, embarked on a remarkable 33-match unbeaten run starting with Nottingham Forest, who were swept aside. A dismal end to 1998 had seen the Reds slip to third in the table behind Villa and Arsenal, but league affairs were put to one side as United's FA Cup adventures began.

Middlesbrough were full of confidence after their 3–2 victory in the last meeting between the two sides and were buoyed further when Andy Townsend gave them the lead.

However, this time United were not to be denied and Andy Cole, Denis Irwin and Ryan Giggs secured Ferguson's men safe passage to Round 4.

A 4–1 thumping of West Ham at Old Trafford continued the blistering start to 1999 and Leicester were on the receiving end of a 6–2 defeat at Filbert Street as the nervous draws that had characterised the start of the season became a distant memory.

The FA Cup served up a tense and tightly-fought battle with rivals Liverpool at Old Trafford with a place in Round 5 at stake. Roy Evans's side took the lead through a Michael Owen header and clung on until the 88th minute, but near constant pressure finally paid dividends as Dwight Yorke struck a priceless equaliser. And Liverpool's misery was compounded in stoppage time when Scholes burst through into the area, with Ole Gunnar Solskjaer taking over and slotting home to win the tie. It was a landmark game in the season and marked a turning point for Scholes and Manchester United. Their 'never say die' attitude was beginning to reap rewards and there was an air of invincibility around the team, with a will and desire to win that no other club would be able to cope with.

Scholes continued his excellent run of form by setting up Dwight Yorke to score the only goal of the game at The Valley as United surged to the top of the league by January.

Returning to the summit of the Premier League was an achievement Scholes was not about to give up lightly, and in an interview with the *Mirror* he said it was the competition they must always strive to win.

'The European Cup is not more important to United than the Premiership,' he said. 'I don't think any of the players think that and I don't think the manager does either. Number one priority is winning the league.'

The cohesion and togetherness displayed by the Manchester United squad in their resurgence in the New Year delighted Scholes, who was happy to share the experience with the players he has grown up with.

'It is even better that so many of us have come through together at club and international level. My aim is to stay in the side. It's great to have a good run and I have been lucky enough to have had that.'

Scholes was afforded a starting place as United hosted Derby at Old Trafford looking to avoid another draw against Jim Smith's struggling side, and they were again indebted to Dwight Yorke for a 65th-minute strike that proved too much for the relegation-haunted Rams. Ole Gunnar Solskjaer confirmed his cult status among the Old Trafford faithful as he netted four goals after coming on as a substitute as Nottingham Forest were on the receiving end of an 8-1 thrashing at the City Ground. Scholes claimed two assists and laid on for the Norwegian hit man to bag his hat-trick in a stunning performance.

Scholes was absent from the United side that edged past Kevin Keegan's Fulham, bolstered by the considerable financial muscle of Mohammad Al Fayed, in the FA Cup, a game that was swiftly followed by the visit of Arsenal to Old Trafford. Nicolas Anelka again proved the scourge of the United defence as he struck a 47th-minute goal to silence the Stretford End, but Andy Cole was on hand to head home a priceless equaliser on the hour mark. Scholes promptly replaced Jesper Blomqvist as Ferguson pushed for all three points, but the Gunners clung on, despite near constant pressure from the rejuvenated Reds.

On 21 February, Paul Scholes tied the knot with his long-term girlfriend Claire Froggatt at Rossett Hall, near Wrexham in the Welsh Borders. The couple were childhood sweethearts, and had been together since the age of 16. United teammates Gary and Phil Neville, Nicky Butt, Ryan Giggs and David Beckham were all in attendance.

Nervous victories over Coventry and Southampton preceded the Champions League quarter-final with Inter Milan, who travelled to Old Trafford looking for a crucial away goal to give them the upper hand in the tie. Scholes continued to be the integral link between the midfield and the blossoming Cole–Yorke partnership, playing in an advanced role knowing Roy Keane would provide ample cover at the back.

It was a dream European night at Old Trafford as two wonderful David Beckham crosses set up Dwight Yorke, who bagged a brace to stun the Milan giants. The Reds rode their luck, however, needing heroics from Peter Schmeichel and Henning Berg to shut out the desperate Inter strikers.

With one foot in the Champions League semi-final, Chelsea came to Old Trafford looking for FA Cup success in an ill-tempered sixth-round tie. Scholes was shown a red card for the only time that season for two innocuous challenges, and was suspended for the replay in west London, where a stunning Yorke chip secured a 2–0 victory and safe passage to the semi-finals of the competition.

Scholes returned to the side for the next league encounter at St James' Park, where Newcastle again hoped to frustrate the champions elect in front of a vocal Toon Army. Scholes admits that St James' Park is a ground where he has always enjoyed playing due to the atmosphere created by the fanatical Geordies.

'I like playing at Newcastle's ground,' he told Manchester United's official website. 'There's always a good atmosphere, the crowd really get behind their team. And we always tend to do well there!'

This time it was Andy Cole at the double as United edged a tight encounter 2–1 in what was perfect preparation for the trip to the San Siro.

Knowing they had to score to be in with a chance of progressing, Inter played their trump card, putting Brazilian striker Ronaldo into the starting line-up despite questions over his fitness. Again United were indebted to Henning Berg for a goal-saving challenge, but they fell behind in the second half when Nicola Ventola slotted past Schmeichel as the tension reached fever pitch in Milan.

With the game delicately poised, Scholes demonstrated his ruthless finishing in the box to win the tie for Ferguson's side. Having ghosted into the area, he collected an Andy Cole header and coolly slid the ball underneath Gianluca Pagliuca to give his side not only a 3–1 lead in the tie, but an away goal too. It proved too much for the Italians, and the Reds advanced to only their second semi-final under Ferguson.

The momentum continued with a routine 3–1 win over Everton, with Gary Neville grabbing a rare goal. A 1–1 draw with Wimbledon was not ideal preparation for the visit of Juventus, but David Beckham was on hand to rescue a point as United cast half an eye on the massive tie in midweek.

Ferguson's men were on the back of an amazing unbeaten run in all competitions but Juventus represented a step up in class. Didier Deschamps and Edgar Davids provided a solid base in the midfield for the mercurial Zinédine Zidane to pull the strings and with Filippo Inzaghi upfront, the United defence could not afford a single lapse in concentration.

Juve's Antonio Conte slotted home to silence Old Trafford and gift the Italians a crucial away goal. In a breathless night of European football, the hosts were denied a penalty and had a Teddy Sheringham header ruled out. But, after Scholes had tussled in the area, the ball broke to Ryan Giggs to lash home the equaliser and leave the semi-final delicately poised at the halfway point.

There was no letup in the club competitions as the Reds met Arsenal at Villa Park for a place in the FA Cup final in May. The game proved to be a scrappy affair, and Roy Keane had his smart volley harshly ruled out, meaning the rivals would have to face off once more.

The replay would prove to be one of the most legendary FA Cup ties of all time. David Beckham's measured strike gave United the lead before Dennis Bergkamp hauled the Gunners level. However, this time Nicolas Anelka suffered the agony of a disallowed goal as the Gunners ran off to celebrate in the crowd prematurely. The game remained on a knife edge until Phil Neville brought down Ray Parlour in injury time, giving Bergkamp the opportunity to win the tie. He failed, as Schmeichel hurled his considerable frame to his left to push the ball away and keep the tie alive.

Extra time was needed to separate the sides and Ryan Giggs chose to take the game by the scruff of the neck. Collecting a wayward pass from Patrick Vieira, he jinked his way through the Arsenal rearguard before striking firmly over Seaman to win the tie.

Scholes had kept pace with Giggs throughout the run and was an option for the square pass after the Welshman had worked his way into the area, but admits he could only watch as one of history's greatest FA Cup goals unfolded before his eyes.

'It was just unbelievable', Scholes said. 'I was asking him to square it – I don't know why and I'm glad he didn't! He just smashed it into the top corner. It was an unbelievable goal and, with the circumstances it was in, it was amazing.'

The upturn in United's fortunes became apparent as they brushed aside Sheffield Wednesday 3–0 to avenge the shock defeat at Hillsborough. Scholes rifled in the third to cap a comfortable victory ahead of another trip to Italy.

With a place in the FA Cup final secured, Manchester United travelled to Turin knowing they needed to score in order to book their place in Barcelona come May. A goalless draw would have been good enough for Juventus, which played into the hands of the defensive-minded Italians. In spite of this they raced to a two-goal lead, thanks to the predatory instincts of the Italian hit man Filippo Inzaghi. Though undoubtedly shell-shocked at the nightmare start, the character of Ferguson's squad shone through as Roy Keane glanced a Beckham corner into the back of the net to haul United back into contention, and, when Yorke made it 2-2 on the night, Manchester United were going through on goal difference. Not satisfied with a draw, United surged forward and Andy Cole made certain of a trip to the Catalan capital as he slid home despite Yorke being felled by Angelo Peruzzi in the build-up.

However, in the 76th minute the referee blew after a typically bullish Scholes challenge and, after questioning the decision, he picked up his second booking of the knockout stages, which meant he would miss the Champions League final, the culmination of football's greatest ever adventure.

'It was a sickening thought when I realised I was going to miss the match in the Nou Camp,' Scholes confessed. 'The final represented the biggest game of my life, even bigger than playing for England.

'Just think of being able to play for the European Cup. I might never get a chance of being there again. I doubt if I will really appreciate just how bad it is until I'm in the Nou Camp and the lads walk out on to the pitch. Then it'll bite really bad. I'll know I could be down there.'

Following their European exertions, Scholes and United were brought down to earth with a 1-1 draw at Elland Road and slipped to second in the league, but with a crucial game in hand that would see them return to the top spot if they won. And the chance came against Aston Villa, whose excellent form in the first half of the season had dipped dramatically. Scholes was on hand with a priceless assist, though Villa defender Steve Watson got the last touch. The Midlands club rallied and drew level through Julian Joachim, who was a thorn in the United side once again, but Beckham was on hand to deliver yet another priceless winning goal.

A nervous win over Villa was followed by a trip to Anfield with the end of the season in sight and, despite a solid performance in front of the vocal Kop, former Red Devil Paul Ince scored a crucial equaliser as a breathless match finished two apiece. The result on Merseyside was followed by disappointing draws with Middlesbrough at The Riverside, but it was enough to see the Reds move top with a game in hand.

Brian Kidd's Blackburn Rovers needed all three points if they were to stave off relegation, but a goalless draw at Ewood Park did little good for either side, meaning that victory at home to Tottenham was a must if United were to secure the first of three trophies inside 11 days.

In what seemed like a feature of the season, the hosts fell behind as Les Ferdinand's looping effort found the back of the net to silence the packed Old Trafford, who were expecting a party atmosphere to finish the league season. Scholes tried to force an equaliser, drawing a miraculous double-save from Ian Walker in the Spurs goal. But he was on hand as United drew level, stealing the ball from Tim Sherwood with a strong challenge before feeding Beckham to fire in the equaliser. The title was secured through a moment of genius from Andy Cole as he collected a high ball with a deft touch, before steadying himself and lobbing Ian Walker with pinpoint accuracy. As Ian Walker punted the ball forward, Scholes won an unchallenged header as the referee blew time on the Premier League season. Cue celebrations across Manchester.

Scholes admits that retaining the Premiership helped alleviate some of the expectation. 'It has taken a bit of pressure off us as we have definitely won something,' he said. 'Now we can just look forward to these two games and hope to win them as well.'

Despite defending the title from Arsenal there was more work to be done, starting with the FA Cup final against Ruud Gullit's Newcastle. Ferguson put his faith in Keane – despite his suspension for the Champions League final – and Scholes at Wembley. Scholes said before the match that he and Keane were eager to secure more domestic success for their teammates.

'Keano and I have to do a job at Wembley by making sure the double is secure,' he said. 'It's the last game for the pair of us and we want to go out on a high by making sure the treble's a possibility too. I think the lads can beat Bayern, so it's up to us to help beat Newcastle.'

Ahead of the match Scholes confessed that their attention was fully focused on beating Newcastle, despite the mammoth task ahead of them in midweek.

'It's a big game, it's the FA Cup Final, regardless of whatever game's coming next,' he said. 'We want to win the game, we want to win trophies, we want to win medals. We're not going to go out and take it easy. It's the FA Cup Final and we want to win it.'

The game proved to be a low-key affair, with the Magpies rarely threatening Peter Schmeichel's goal. Roy Keane had to be withdrawn with an ankle injury and his replacement – Teddy Sheringham – opened the scoring. Scholes was instrumental in the gradual dismantling of the Geordies and his assist for Sheringham's opener was sublime. Feigning a shot on the edge of the area, he guided a measured pass through to Sheringham, who slotted underneath Steve Harper. Sheringham then turned provider as he fed Scholes to fire in from inside the area to settle the contest and leave Manchester United one game away from football heaven. After his match-winning performance, Scholes spoke of his delight at playing underneath the Twin Towers.

'Wembley is becoming a bit of a lucky ground for me,' he said. 'It's not bad to follow a hat-trick for England with a goal in the FA Cup Final. I don't think Newcastle got a kick. We had just won the league the week before and it was a huge game. It was played really well that day and it could have been four or five, really, and it was a nice, comfortable win.'

And he was typically modest regarding the strike. He said, 'It wasn't one of my best. I didn't hit the ball cleanly, but I got just enough on it. That's my only Cup final goal for United and it was amazing. Another medal in Barcelona would finish off a great season for both me and the club.'

In the absence of the two first-choice central midfielders, Scholes's youth team friend and roommate Nicky Butt was asked to slot in alongside David Beckham. Scholes spoke of his delight at sharing his ascent to global superstardom with Butt: 'So many of us have come through together at club and international level. I've roomed with Nicky ever since I can remember. We've been mates for years and it's brilliant that we've grown up together and are playing for United and England.'

With the domestic legs of the fabled treble now in place, Manchester United travelled to Barcelona knowing they were ninety minutes away from footballing history. For Scholes – and midfield partner Roy Keane – the occasion would be laced with regret and frustration at knowing they would be unable to take part in the biggest game in almost half a century.

'I felt almost as sorry for Scholesy as for myself,' Keane said in his autobiography. 'He was arguably the most gifted player in our squad. Missing this must hurt him so badly, especially after seeing all his mates from the 1992 and 1993 Youth Cup final teams playing for the ultimate prize in the European game.'

But the United skipper admits that being in the same position as Scholes helped him work through the pain of missing the match at the Nou Camp.

'Paul was the perfect pro,' Keane continued. 'Superb on the field, modest and sensible off it. No celebrity bullshit, no self-promotion of glory hunting, an amazingly gifted player who remained an unaffected human being. Oddly, the fact that he and I were in the same boat took the edge off my disappointment.'

Manchester United's team hotel overlooked the sea in Sitges, and, with no preparation for the forthcoming battle required,

Scholes and Keane spent time with fans in the hotel's bar hoping to occupy their minds, and not dwell on the disappointment of missing the game. The European Cup Final against Bayern Munich, 41 years in the waiting, got off to a nightmare start as Mario Basler's weak free kick found a gap in the Manchester United wall to gift the Germans the lead after just three minutes. After this both sides cancelled each other out as the game increasingly turned into a battle in the middle of the park, where Scholes and Keane would have relished the tussle against Bayern's midfield enforcer, Stefan Effenberg.

What happened next is the most dramatic finish to a European Cup final in history, as Sheringham and Solskjaer netted in injury time to break Munich hearts and send the travelling Mancunians into raptures. The one trophy that had dodged Alex Ferguson throughout his managerial career was now coming back to Old Trafford. While Sam Kuffour and Lothar Matthaus lay broken and sobbing on the grass, the men in Red celebrated their breathtaking victory. Scholes and Keane, still dressed in their grey Cup final suits, were given a guard of honour by their teammates as they lifted the trophy in front of the jubilant United fans at the Nou Camp.

The city was awash with red, white and black as Mancunians took over a square off Las Ramblas, and celebrated long into the night in Barcelona.

In the 1998–99 season, Scholes scored 11 goals, with 11 yellow cards and one red. His goals total was modest by his standards but the timing and impact of his performances helped steer Manchester United to the greatest season in their history.

Match-winning displays against Liverpool at Old Trafford and against Newcastle in the FA Cup final secured Scholes's place as one of the first names on Sir Alex Ferguson's team sheet. Rather than rest on their successes, and be content with their remarkable achievements, Manchester United would fight and scrap to hold onto their Premier League title into the new millennium, despite Arsène Wenger plotting to overthrow the Kings of English and European football.

Chapter 4

STRIVING
FOR MORE

'I would be very surprised if we won it by the same margin again.'
PAUL SCHOLES

Ferguson resisted the temptation to disrupt his treble-winning side by cashing in on their success – and signing a host of foreign names hungry for glory. With a midfield quartet of Giggs, Scholes, Keane and Beckham, the Scot had little need to invest heavily to change a team that had dominated domestic and European football the previous term. Scholes had grown into his midfield role and would continue to prove his worth to Manchester United in the 1999–2000 season, as the Premier League moved into the new millennium on the crest of a Red wave.

Scholes missed United's pre-season tour abroad, as his wife Claire was heavily pregnant with their first child. He spent his pre-season in Manchester whipping the reserve side into shape, while keeping his mobile phone close to hand. Sir Alex Ferguson had told him to put family first at this time, but he was able to make the season's curtain raiser at Wembley. Early bragging rights, however, would belong to Arsenal as they edged a tepid Charity Shield 2–1 on 1 August. Scholes played the full ninety minutes in the Wembley contest but goals from Kanu and Ray Parlour brought victory for Arsène Wenger's side.

Paul and Claire were soon celebrating the birth of their son Aiden, capping an almost perfect year for the midfield star both on and off the pitch.

When the season started a week later, many expected United to come tearing out off the blocks, but a dogged and determined Everton earned a 1–1 draw to frustrate the champions. However, they would not have to wait long for their first win – and Scholes his first goal of the season – against Sheffield Wednesday. The United midfielder netted inside ten minutes to open the floodgates at Old Trafford – with the home side strolling to a 4–0 win. United continued their fine form with wins over Leeds and – more importantly – Arsenal before travelling to Coventry City for a match many expected them to win comfortably.

While United were beginning to show they were a class above many in England's top division, they required some Scholes magic to see off Gordon Strachan's side at Highfield Road. Having found the net on the hour mark through Scholes, Dwight Yorke was on hand to double the advantage before a John Aloisi goal against the run of play made United squirm during the final few minutes.

Being champions of Europe gave United the right to contest

the European Super Cup, against UEFA Cup winners Lazio in Monaco's concrete jungle – the Stade Louis II. United never really threatened the Rome club in a disappointing match in the South of France, with one-time United target Marcelo Salas netting the only goal to earn Lazio the trophy.

United remained unbeaten throughout September beating Liverpool, Sturm Graz and Marseille, while being held by Dynamo Zagreb, Wimbledon and Southampton. Near neighbours Leeds United were keeping the pressure up at the top of the table, as David O'Leary's young side continued to take the Premier League by storm – with a series of United draws handing the Yorkshire side the top spot. The club had been going strongly in defence of their European crown but were indebted to match winner Scholes in their clash with the powerful French side Marseille. Having fallen behind to Ibrahim Bakayoko's goal, Andy Cole hit back with a quarter of an hour remaining before Scholes settled the match on 83 minutes.

October brought mixed fortunes for United, as a Jekyll-and-Hyde month saw some big scorelines – though not all in the Reds' favour. On 3 October they were humbled at Chelsea, finally succumbing to a 5–0 victory in west London. With Scholes's midfield partner Nicky Butt being dismissed, it handed Chelsea a massive advantage – and a Gus Poyet brace set them on their way to a massive win in the capital.

United were able to take out their frustrations on Premier League newcomers Watford in the next league fixture – and restored some pride with a 4–1 win over the hapless Hornets. Defeats at Marseille and Tottenham disrupted any sort of United rhythm as the season began to settle down – but Scholes was on hand to bag another goal at the end of the month as the Reds cruised past Aston Villa by three goals. United were becoming increasingly reliant on the goals of Andy Cole, and the England striker again proved his worth in the win over Leicester.

Scholes was a major factor in England's playoff victory over Scotland to book their place in the European Championships taking place in the summer, with Kilmarnock manager Alex Totten admitting he attempted an audacious move for Scholes when he was an unknown reserve player – only to be laughed off by Ferguson.

'I went to watch Neil Whitworth and Colin McKee playing but Scholes caught my eye,' he told Scotland's *Daily Record*. 'He scored a couple of goals in a 3–0 win and I thought he was just what we needed in midfield. Alex Ferguson wasn't at the game but told me to give him a ring later after I'd seen it. I told him I was happy to sign McKee and Whitworth, but what about the boy Scholes?'

Totten continued, 'He just started laughing and said, "He's a bit special, all of them are." They were tremendous that night and the potential was there for all to see. The rest, as they say, is history. Alex added that I'd be hearing a lot more about the boys in the squad and he was absolutely right as usual. There they are as European champions.

'I actually felt for Scholes missing the final against Bayern Munich because he helped them get there but I think he'll have more chances in his career to play in European Cup final. Scholes is a fantastic wee player and I thought he was man of the match in every sense at Hampden, quite apart from the goals. He knows when to pass, when to hold, when to run and when to shoot. A midfielder who can time his runs into the box is worth his weight in gold.'

So Scholes was denied the chance to move north of the border, and instead lined up to take part in the Toyota Cup, contested between the European champions and Brazilian side Palmeiras in Japan. Ferguson knew he could not take a full squad across to the Far East, so settled for a squad of 18, with Scholes one of the players set to travel.

'We're looking forward to it, and I think Palmeiras will be treating it as their biggest game of the year,' Ferguson said ahead of the game. 'An English team has never won the tournament, so it places importance on Manchester United. We're very serious about winning this because it's the world club championship, and, when this kind of situation presents itself, it is the culture of this club that we have got to win it.'

And United duly wrote their name in the history books with a 1–0 win over the South Americans.

Buoyed by the win, United went into the Christmas period as champions of world club football and celebrated with crushing wins over Everton, Valencia, West Ham and Bradford to finish 1999 in stunning form. United totalled sixteen goals in those four wins, with Scholes finding the back of the net against Valencia in the Champions League.

With both England and Manchester United requiring Scholes's services, there were competing interests regarding the midfielder, who desperately needed a hernia operation. If United could not afford to lose him until the summer, England would miss out when contesting the European Championships in Holland and Belgium.

'We might not have to consider the question of an operation until the season is over,' said Ferguson. 'Paul is feeling better and the original problem has eased. He hasn't been complaining about it recently and isn't suffering pain any more,' he told the *Evening Standard*. Scholes had played through the pain on a number of occasions but his manager accepted the fact that the operation – and a lengthy layoff – could not be avoided.

United caused countrywide furore at the end of the year by agreeing to take part in the inaugural Club World Championships in Brazil at the start of 2000. United were under pressure from the Football Association to take part in the competition to improve their standing on the world stage – which was vitally important if England was to mount a bid to host the World Cup in the coming years. However, taking part in the tournament would involve pulling out of the FA Cup, football's oldest competition – an idea that was unthinkable for many.

Scholes, meanwhile, would not travel to South America, as the need for the hernia operation took precedence, as confirmed by the United boss. We won't take Paul to Brazil,' Ferguson told the *Daily Express*. 'He will see a specialist in the next few days and hopefully everything will be sorted out while we are competing in the World Club Championship.'

The tournament (now known as the FIFA Club World Cup) proved to be a woeful exercise for the Reds, as Mexican side Necaxa and Brazilians Vasco da Gama proved much more suited to the heat – sending United home with their pride severely bruised.

Scholes returned from his layoff on 29 January for a game against Middlesbrough, which saw United finally reclaim top spot in the league. With Scholes in the side, United would maintain a 100 per cent record in the league for the remainder of the season, picking up 14 straight wins when the flame-headed midfielder took part. Scholes scored eight goals in the winning run, with his first coming against Coventry City at Old Trafford – where the Reds edged a tight encounter 3–2.

United were unstoppable going into March, and Scholes netted once more against Bradford, as Ferguson's side completed a comprehensive double over the Yorkshire side with a 4–0 win. However, it was on 1 April that Scholes played his joker – and netted his first hat-trick for Manchester United in their 7–1 mauling of West Ham. The result almost guaranteed the title and Ferguson pointed out that Leeds now faced an uphill battle.

'That has made it difficult for Leeds now, but they have still done well and had a great season,' he told the *Sunday Mirror* after the game. 'But we have had one of those days when everything has gone right – we've been threatening this type of result for a few weeks now. It was a performance that you can't help feeling delighted about. To start with, our work rate was magnificent and that gave us the foundation to show our ability. The important thing now is that the players enjoy themselves. I reckon we need another three or four wins to ensure the title but we've got to try to win the lot.'

Of Scholes's goal glut, Ferguson said, 'We've been waiting a long time for Paul to do that, and I'm so pleased for him.' All bets were now off as United looked to have landed their sixth league title despite plenty of matches left in the season, but such was the champions' sumptuous form that mangers up and down the country were throwing in the towel. 'I would say Manchester United are now uncatchable,' Chelsea boss Gianluca Vialli said after the match, 'which is a shame, as there are seven games left. It is now exhibition matches for them.'

Chelsea had all but ended Leeds's title challenge with victory at Stamford Bridge, thanks to young substitute John Harley. Manchester United's thumping win over the Hammers proved perfect preparation for United's Champions League quarter-final with Real Madrid in defence of their crown. The Spanish giants would pose a great threat to the European Kings, having won the title more times than any other club. The first leg took place in Madrid's Santiago Bernabéu stadium, and Ferguson could boast a full-strength side to face off against Raul, Fernando Morientes, Roberto Carlos and co. Despite the wealth of attacking flair on offer, the match ended in a goalless draw, handing United home advantage for the decisive second leg.

In between the two ties United had to negotiate two tricky league fixtures. The first, a clash with Middlesbrough, posed the greater threat as United continued to inch their way to domestic glory. Scholes scored yet again as United edged a 4–3 win over the Teessiders, all but securing the league title. In their next encounter, with Sunderland – which United won by four goals to nil – they surpassed the Premier League's highest goal-total record.

After the win, United had amassed 84 goals and were 14 points above second-placed Liverpool. However, with the title all but secure, United's season now hinged on the outcome of the Old Trafford clash with Real Madrid, and United surrendered their European crown with barely a whimper – having been blown away by their Spanish counterparts by three goals to one. Scholes's late penalty could not galvanise United into a comeback, as Real stormed through to the semi-finals with a comprehensive victory.

'It's a shock to me because I thought we had an outstanding chance,' Ferguson said after the game. 'I have no excuses because Real Madrid were the better team on the night. Their keeper, Casillas, produced some marvellous saves. It just isn't normal for an eighteen-year-old goalkeeper to show that sort of consistency of form. The own goal in the first half left us chasing the game and the two we conceded after that were poor goals on our part.

'We could have shown more caution at the start of the second half but I suppose that's not in the nature of this team, as they want to get situations back, and I have no criticism of them for that. Real surprised me playing with three at the back and we should have sorted that situation out quickly. I still think we had a lot of great attacking play but it just wasn't our night. It's hard to believe, because I really thought we could have done it.'

All that was now left for United was to see out the remainder of the Premier League season to retain their domestic crown. Not entered into the FA Cup, and with the League Cup slipping out of their grasp, United were at least guaranteed some silverware – but they were unable to build on their remarkable success of last term, and a single trophy did not represent true growth in the United side.

With Scholes in the side, United picked up nine points from three games against Chelsea, Tottenham and Aston Villa to win the league at a canter – a massive 18-point margin. After victory over Tottenham at Old Trafford the United players circled the Old Trafford pitch, clutching their loved ones, and Scholes introduced ten-month-old son Aaron to the turf that had made him a star in front of a record attendance at the Theatre of Dreams. Scholes headed off to the summer's European championships with the Premier League safely locked away in the Old Trafford trophy room, hoping to fire his country to success as well.

While Scholes and England endured a mediocre summer in Holland and Belgium, Ferguson had been busy making small changes to his squad in order to improve on their disappointing European campaign the previous season. Australian goalkeeper Mark Bosnich had failed to make the number-one jersey his own after Peter Schmeichel's retirement – and was replaced by French World Cup winner Fabien Barthez. French defender Mikael Silvestre also joined from Inter Milan to add another defensive option in the absence of stalwart Denis Irwin.

Scholes had signed a new long-term deal with Manchester United to end speculation of a move aboard. His 18 goals last term had raised his stock in Italy and Spain, with most of Europe's elite clubs said to be interested in the England international. But, with his focus now back with Manchester United, Scholes was quick to play down their chances of running away with the title once again.

'We're always confident even if we haven't won the title in the previous season,' he said. 'But I'd be very surprised if we won it by the same margin again. I don't think anyone will win it by eighteen points again. We always seem to mention a few teams like Chelsea, Liverpool and Leeds, but I would have thought Arsenal will be our main threat. Our aims for the season are obviously to win the league and do better in the European Cup in hopefully a couple of steps further than last time.

'It's a very good tournament to be involved in,' he continued. 'The teams are all good ones, and I don't think there's another pre-season competition with as much high quality. It's nice that we're only flying for a couple of hours rather than travelling halfway round the world, because it takes it out of you. Our aims for the season are obviously to win the league and do better in the European Cup – hopefully a couple of steps further than last time.'

Inter Milan had long courted Paul Scholes, but David Beckham was another player apparently heading for the United exit door. Club captain Roy Keane, no stranger to transfer speculation himself, admitted that anything could happen when talking about Europe's best players. 'As far as I'm aware neither of them is unhappy. But I'm not naïve enough to think that things don't change,' he said. 'There's always the possibility of players being tapped up. And it's bound to get players thinking if they can double or treble what they're earning now.'

With Real Madrid, Barcelona and even Lazio backed by seemingly limitless coffers, football wages and transfer fees began to spiral, and Keane admits that even United could not compete with the Continent's biggest spenders.

'We would love to have a Figo, Zidane or a Rivaldo at United but the players don't really think about them because they realise they are never going to come here,' he said.

Real Madrid left the footballing world dumbfounded when they shelled out £38 million for Luís Figo, but, according to Keane, he was worth every penny. 'Figo is an absolutely outstanding player and, if you ask my opinion, he was quite cheap at the price. I can't speak highly enough of him – he's up there with Zidane and Rivaldo as the best three midfielders in the world.'

Scholes, meanwhile, could never be tempted with a move away from Old Trafford – unless Oldham ever came knocking. United had been due to spend big, with prolific PSV striker Ruud van Nistelrooy due at Old Trafford, only to rupture cruciate knee ligaments when on the verge of inking an £18 million deal at Old Trafford. Scholes was defiant in the face of big-money moves, insisting United's reliance on youth would serve them well.

'All the young lads love the club and want to stay here,' he said at the launch of a new Nike football. 'When you come from the area it means so much more. We know what Manchester United means to so many people and we all want to be there as long as we can. I've been here for nine years, since I left school at sixteen. I'm twenty-five now and getting old, but I don't think I'll be getting a testimonial for a while. However, I would like to be here until I finish playing and I think it's the same for all the young lads who have come through.'

However, with massive sums of money now commonplace in football, Scholes admitted it was a concern that one day United could be tempted to accept a huge offer for his services. 'You do get frightened that one day they might snatch their hand off,' he said, 'but we're certainly at least on a par with any other club. These days, there aren't many players who stay at one club. They are all off making all the money, turning up one year here and then somewhere else. But we all want to stay together and be part of a successful United for years to come. Me, Becks, Nicky, Ryan, the Nevilles – we all feel the same.'

Having grown up with the same players, and many coming from Manchester, Scholes admitted they had more feeling and affection for the club than many expensive summer imports could understand. And, with Manchester City now back in the Premier League after flirting with ruin in the lower divisions, Scholes admitted that he was happy to see them back in the big time.

'I do think City will stay up and I'm glad they came back up. But only because of those derby matches – I'm not a City fan by any means!'

United met FA Cup winners Chelsea in the Community Shield, the last time it would be contested underneath the famous twin towers, with Wembley due to be demolished later in the year. United were once again to be found wanting in the curtain raiser, as the west London side eased to a 2–0 win, compounded by Roy Keane's second-half dismissal. However, once the season got under way, it was business as usual, with United strolling past Newcastle at Old Trafford thanks to Ronny Johnson and Andy Cole. However, disappointing draws against Ipswich Town and West Ham saw United move into September with a lack of cutting edge, proving unable to kill off sides they would have expected to beat comfortably. But any rumours of United's demise proved premature as they romped past Bradford 6–0 at Old Trafford in a performance that underlined their dominance of the league.

There was no letup, as Scholes bagged a brace in the next league game against Sunderland, steering United towards a 3–0 win. United's free-scoring form continued in Europe, as Belgian side Anderlecht proved scant opposition for the Reds, who eased to a 5–1 win thanks largely to the efforts of the resurgent Andy Cole, and remained in cruise control in the 3–1 win over Everton. With September coming to a close, United met stern opposition from Chelsea, and the two sides shared a six-goal thriller, with Scholes netting after a quarter of an hour to cancel out Jimmy-Floyd Hasselbaink's opener.

Scholes found the net in the next match, a Champions League encounter with PSV, but United went down to a 3–1 win in Eindhoven. United needed to return to form fast ahead of their trip to Arsenal on 1 October, but it was Arsène Wenger's side who inflicted a first league defeat for the Reds, picking up all three points courtesy of Thierry Henry's wonder goal. United got their revenge for their 3–1 humbling in Holland by winning by the same margin in the return fixture at Old Trafford – with Scholes once again among the goals. A morale-boosting 3–0 win over Leeds followed before a stunning defeat to Anderlecht in Belgium. United bounced back from the defeat by thumping five past Southampton as the gulf in class between European and domestic competition became too great to ignore.

Roy Keane accused many of United's players of resting on their laurels after the treble-winning season, and failing to push on and strive for more with their names already etched in the history books. With two straight league titles, with a third looking increasingly likely, United needed to find an extra gear when competing on the Continent if they were to consider themselves European greats alongside Real Madrid, AC Milan and Ajax. The 1998–99 season may have capped Ferguson's greatest spell as United boss, but his club captain wanted more and questioned whether many of his teammates shared the drive and hunger for success.

Keane spoke in his autobiography of United's failure to capitalise on their successes of that season:

We should have bought big after the treble, been ruthless, got the best in Europe, freshened things up, attacked complacency, let anyone who really didn't care if they ever won another trophy leave to join the king of clubs that never win any trophies. Maybe this team has had it.

United continued to power towards the league title, but the club needed Champions League success to consider themselves true greats. On a personal level, Scholes bagged 12 goals during the 2000–01 season, not his best tally but a fair return for a midfielder. Arsenal, the club's greatest challengers to the Premier League crown, were thumped 6–1 at Old Trafford as United underlined their dominance of the domestic game. Roy Keane hit a stunning hat-trick as the Gunners were well and truly blown away.

However, Europe presented an entirely different proposition.

United had fought their way to the quarter-finals of the Champions League but were bested by Bayern Munich over two legs. United won the league at a canter, by ten points, and celebrated after a lacklustre defeat to Derby County – a meaningless match when the title had already been won.

Meanwhile, in the summer Paul Scholes celebrated the birth of his second child, a daughter named Alisha, in early May.

Chapter 5

LIFE AFTER FERGUSON?

*'Do you want to go on? Do you want to show why you won
all those medals? That is the pertinent question.'*
SIR ALEX FERGUSON

Sir Alex Ferguson had announced that this would be his last
season at the helm of Manchester United – a decision that
shook the club to its core and sent fans across the country into
mourning. However, after the club had won the Premier League
three times running, the Manchester United faithful were
becoming complacent with domestic glory, while frustration at
their European failings cast a shadow over any success since the
magnificent treble-winning season. In his autobiography, Roy
Keane lamented the lack of hunger at Old Trafford, claiming the
players lost their drive since winning the Champions League two
years previously.

Paul Scholes signed a six-year contract in early July, along
with Nicky Butt, who put pen to paper on a five-year deal which

would double their current wages at the club. In order to stop the apparent rot, the United board spent big in the summer, acquiring Argentine playmaker Juan Verón for £28.5 million, while Dutch hit man Ruud van Nistelrooy finally overcame his year-long injury nightmare to ink a lucrative contract at the club. The acquisition of Verón, a classy attacking midfielder, put him in direct competition with Scholes for a midfield berth alongside Roy Keane. Ferguson attempted to overcome this problem by pushing Scholes further forward, playing as a second striker behind Ruud van Nistelrooy.

With the new signings bringing intense competition for places in the side, Ferguson hoped the newcomers would restore the hunger at Old Trafford. 'The worst fear for any top player at my club is their Manchester United place will be taken away from them,' he is quoted as saying in the *Sun*. 'Hopefully the new signings will have the desired effect. Without question we had to get them because I could see what was happening on the pitch last season.

'I believe the players got it into their minds that we were never going to buy another big player. I know there were some of them who wanted that new challenge of fresh faces. I wouldn't say they were in a comfort zone last season because I see enough of them in training to know that is not the case but, unwittingly, when you have effectively won the league by January, the edge can come off your play.'

Scholes was widely regarded as England's finest all-round midfielder and Ferguson hinted in pre-season of his plans to utilise him in a more advanced position.

'In Paul Scholes we have a player who, without question, can score at any level,' he said. 'He's only one behind Andy Cole in our European standings. But he only scored seven in the league last season. Quite a lot of times he's tried to shore up the midfield to the detriment of his other qualities. Hopefully, with the maturity of the players we have he will use his talent a bit more.'

Andy Cole and Dwight Yorke were two players who had never quite recaptured the form of the 1998–99 season and Ferguson's statement piled the pressure on the two strikers. 'A player of Paul Scholes's ability may have the chance to try new things this season,' Ferguson told the *Manchester Evening News*. 'But you have to remember that he started here as a striker who played off the front two. He will have a part to play but the thought of Verón and Keane playing together in midfield is awesome. I expect us to be so powerful in that department this year.'

While Verón came with a tremendous track record in international football and Italy's Serie A, Scholes was being forced out of his favoured position to accommodate the Argentinian – causing a few to raise eyebrows. Former United youth team player Jonathan Greening, who was limited to cameo appearances in the first team, accused the club of going against the youth policy that had been the foundation of all their previous success.

'The club is more likely to spend millions rather than give fringe players the chance to establish themselves,' he said in Newcastle's *Evening Chronicle*. 'I have a Champions League winner's medal after sitting on the bench when we beat Bayern. But I didn't play a single minute of European football that season. I felt a bit of a fraud when I got the medal.'

Any upheaval in the Old Trafford dressing room was put to one side for the Charity Shield match against Liverpool, where Scholes started as a second striker behind Ruud van Nistelrooy. Verón, who was away on international duty, missed the match, with Nicky Butt occupying the other slot in central midfield. Scholes went close with a number of efforts, but was left frustrated by the inspired Sander Westerveld. Liverpool took a pulsating match 2–1 as Ferguson's new formation failed to reap instant rewards.

The league season started on 19 August with the visit of runaway Division 1 winners Fulham, fuelled by Mohammad Al Fayed's millions. Scholes again started upfront, this time with Phil Neville and Juan Verón playing in central midfield, with Beckham and Giggs working the flanks. United were rocked when their newly promoted opponents took the lead on four minutes through French striker Louis Saha. Beckham hauled the hosts level only for Saha to bag a second shortly after the interval. Ruud van Nistelrooy then went some way to repaying his £19 million transfer fee with two goals in as many minutes to give United a 3–2 win in a breathless opener.

Successive draws with Blackburn Rovers and Aston Villa marked a nervy start to the season. Scholes was forced out of the side that swept to a 4–1 win over Everton, which moved United up to third in the table before a fiery encounter with Newcastle at St James' Park. Scholes did not warrant a starting place, with Ferguson opting for a midfield pairing of Verón and Keane, with Andy Cole partnering van Nistelrooy in attack. He replaced Cole on 59 minutes with United 3–1 down and the move brought instant rewards, as goals from Giggs and Verón in quick succession hauled United level. However, a Wes Brown own goal ten minutes from time sparked an ugly confrontation in injury time, when Roy Keane was sent off for aiming a punch at goading Newcastle star Alan Shearer.

After the match Scholes admitted the new attacking pairing was far from potent. 'Sometimes it's not so bad and sometimes it's not very good,' he said. 'I think we will tell if it's going to work. I don't think it's gone great so far, but hopefully it can get better. It's quite obvious the way Ruud plays that he wants to score goals and he makes runs in behind defenders. It's up to me to find him and hopefully I can start doing that.'

With Ferguson's impending retirement, this season represented the Scot's last assault on the Champions League, and the Reds' line-up for their opening group game against Lille at Old Trafford. Ferguson opted for the van Nistelrooy–Scholes partnership upfront but once again United were unable to fire on all cylinders, needing a last-gasp goal from David Beckham to steal all three points.

Ferguson fielded a much-changed United side for the visit of Ipswich in the next league encounter on 22 September, with no starting place for Scholes, Verón or van Nistelrooy. Young winger Luke Chadwick and South African Quentin Fortune played down the flanks while Andy Cole and Ole Gunnar Solskjaer were given the opportunity to stake a claim in attack.

Injury-time goals from the striker partnership put the icing on a 4–0 victory, with Scholes replacing Chadwick just after the hour mark to steer the home side to a comfortable win.

Scholes bagged his first goal for United that season as United travelled to Estadio Riazor to face a dangerous and resurgent Deportivo La Coruña boasting plenty of firepower with their striking duo Roy Makaay and Diego Tristán. Scholes struck into the top corner five minutes before half time to silence the Riazor Stadium and bag his 16th Champions League goal for the club. However, United, so often the beneficiaries of late drama, were undone by goals in the closing minutes from Walter Pandiani and Nouredine Naybet as Deportivo fought back to win the match.

In the absence of Ryan Giggs, Ferguson tried a new midfield combination with Beckham, Scholes, Verón and Nicky Butt operating behind van Nistelrooy and Cole in attack. The shift in tactics proved to the detriment of the side in their following league game against Spurs, who raced to a 3–0 lead at half-time with goals from Dean Richards, Les Ferdinand and Christian Ziege. Solskjaer replaced Butt before the interval, with United needing more firepower if they were to get anything from the game. Andy Cole netted within a minute of the restart to give the visitors a glimmer of hope, which was doubled through Lauren Blanc on the hour mark. Goals from van Nistelrooy and Verón hauled United ahead before Beckham's 87th-minute strike – sealing a remarkable 5–3 victory for United as the White Hart Lane crowd watched in horror.

With Manchester United's wealth of attacking options finally firing in unison, Ferguson admitted there could have been a cricket score. 'My players needed to rediscover what they are all about,' he told the *News of the World*. 'They are the best players in the country and they need to show it. We played sometimes like it was a practice match – you score and we will score – and we could have had a lot of goals. It was fantastic, being part of something like that – it was a remarkable performance and a result.'

Ferguson reverted to his favoured formation in Europe for the trip to Olympiakos, with Scholes moving forward to play alongside van Nistelrooy once again. Second-half goals from Beckham and Cole marked a comfortable win against the gritty Greeks, who boasted a formidable home record in the competition. United continued their form in front of goal with a 3-1 win over Sunderland at the Stadium of Light before having the chance for redemption against Deportivo at Old Trafford. Van Nistelrooy had fired United to a seventh-minute lead before Sergio Gonzalez and Diego Tristán hit back. The Dutch striker restored parity before half-time only for Tristán to seal the win on the hour mark.

Scholes was replaced by Andy Cole shortly after the Spanish international's goal, as his front two again failed to connect. However, despite the introduction of Cole, there was no way big into the game for the hosts, who succumbed to a devastating European defeat at Old Trafford. The blip continued as United lost further ground in the league with defeat to Bolton at Old Trafford before breezing past Olympiakos 3-0.

Successive draws with Leeds and Lille caused many to doubt Ferguson's new tactics in what could be his last season in charge at the club. Their misery was compounded by a 3-1 loss to bitter rivals Liverpool, where Scholes was dropped after voicing his thoughts about the new role at the start of November. Defeat by the same margin to Arsenal in the league continued the disastrous run of form for Ferguson's side. United had been in contention for a rare Highbury win before two catastrophic errors from Fabien Barthez gifted the game to Wenger's Gunners. The French international, who many had hoped could finally fill the boots of Peter Schmeichel, had looked unconvincing between the sticks and his erratic nature had drawn criticism from the media.

After the game, Scholes leapt to the defence of the French World Cup winner. 'It's ridiculous to suggest the players have lost faith in Fabien,' he said. 'He's a great keeper and everyone's behind him. He's a very confident man and he'll come back from this even stronger. He doesn't let it get to him and he'll still try things that other keepers won't do.

'Everyone makes mistakes but it's the keeper's errors that get highlighted. I have the ball away and could easily have been punished – but it ended with Fabien making a good save. We're making too many mistakes and we're all as guilty as one another. People are always going to have a go when we aren't playing well – and we aren't playing well. But we don't take much notice of the critics. We will listen to what the manager says and try to come out of this that way.'

The slump continued with a 3–0 defeat to Chelsea as United and Scholes struggled to get to grips with the new formation being imposed upon them. There was to be some respite with a 3–0 win over Boavista in the Champions League but domestically they continued to struggle, losing 1–0 at home to West Ham courtesy of a Jermaine Defoe strike.

Scholes's increasing frustration at his new role within the club came to the boil when he refused to play for in a League Cup tie against Arsenal on 5 November, a game United's youngsters went on to lose 4–0. However, despite the difference of opinion, which came into the public domain, Scholes later said there is always a chance for forgiveness with Sir Alex Ferguson.

'If you apologise, go and see him and talk to him, there is always room to forgive. This is the biggest club in the world and if you lose two or three games it's a crisis. But he is so used to it now that he doesn't let anything faze him or any criticisms affect him.'

Scholes was fined £80,000 for refusing to board the coach to Highbury, a stunning outburst from the normally reserved man, but such was his frustration at the time that there were even rumours of his departure from Old Trafford. The likes of Juventus and Real Madrid were said to be monitoring the situation closely, in case the midfielder's position at the club became untenable. David Beckham, who had fallen foul of Ferguson's wrath more than most at Old Trafford, believed Scholes would come back even stronger in the face of adversity.

'There won't be a problem with Scholesy,' he is quoted as saying in the Belfast News Letter. 'He is a strong character and a big-game player. He has proved that over the years. I don't think there is any chance of him leaving Old Trafford. I don't think Scholesy is down, I have not seen any signs of that. I don't think there is any lifting that needs to be done.

'We are all frustrated as we are not playing as well as we can do and we know that, but there is not a problem in the

Manchester United ranks. People might be terming it as a crisis but then there's supposed to be a crisis every week.'

The imminent departure of Ferguson was one of a few factors that explained United's astonishing dip in form, but Beckham said his hunger was as insatiable as ever.

'The desire of all the players is always massive and that comes from the manager,' he continued. 'I don't think anyone can question his hunger in football. People question our hunger before the start of every season when we have won something and we always proved them wrong. We would have liked this season to be smooth for the manager but I suppose we have to make it hard for ourselves and him.'

Scholes, who had been prolific from midfield so far, had seen the goals dry up despite adopting a more attacking position. If Ferguson had been hoping for the players to show their hunger and desire, now was the time for them to do it.

'Motivation has never been a problem,' the Scot is quoted in the *People* as saying. 'The players' pride has got them where they are. But that is the question now. We will have to say to them now – do you want to go on? Do you want to show why you won all those medals? That is the pertinent question.'

Referring to the devastating 3–1 defeat to Liverpool, Ferguson said, 'I never want to see a Manchester United team go down as easily as that again. The important thing is to make sure that we start playing as a team again and start playing for the right to play for Manchester United. I think that is important. Winning is the best recipe in terms of regaining confidence and it doesn't just apply to Manchester United, it applies to every human being on earth. They have enjoyed winning in the past and, hopefully, they can regroup and find themselves again.'

Liverpool, who had found league success hard to come by since the Premier League's conception, were enjoying an excellent start to their campaign – including their crushing victory over United a few weeks before.

The tough games were coming thick and fast for United, who couldn't climb above sixth place in the table by late November. Despite being five points off, the pace Scholes sent out a message of intent to their title rivals. 'There are still a lot of points to play for yet and even if Liverpool win their game in hand, I wouldn't rule us out yet,' he fired in the *Liverpool Echo*. 'We need to get on a run. All the players know that and hopefully it will start this Saturday. The players are all determined it will start this week.'

Whatever was going on behind the scenes at Old Trafford, publicly Scholes threw his weight behind Ferguson's tactical shift. 'It has been difficult because a lot of people have had their say about the way I am playing and whether that is down to tactics,' he continued 'It's not about tactics, it is about my form. And, to be honest, the tactics aren't all that different. On paper the position should be made for me, but for one reason or another it hasn't really worked.'

By December Scholes had dropped back into midfield as United finally found top gear with a five-goal rout of hapless Derby County. David Beckham was sacrificed to accommodate a midfielder quartet of Scholes, Keane, Verón and Butt – while Solskjaer partnered van Nistelrooy in attack. The Norwegian striker opened the scoring and bagged his second after Roy Keane had doubled the advantage. Van Nistelrooy made it four on the hour mark before Scholes found the net minutes from time. While United's midfield offered little in the way of width, a powerful core proved more than enough to ease past the Rams at Old Trafford. A narrow victory over Middlesbrough was followed by a 6–1 demolition of Southampton, with van Nistelrooy bagging a hat-trick to down the Saints. Wide men Beckham and Giggs both came off the bench with the points already safe, but Scholes, back in his favoured central midfield position, had become an influence in matches once again.

United continued with another four straight victories over the Christmas period as Fulham, Aston Villa, Newcastle, Southampton and Blackburn all fell as the season moved into the New Year.

In the first match of 2002, Paul Scholes bagged a second-half brace at Old Trafford to break his shy spell in front of goal. The win put United back into second spot in the lead, after they had stormed up the table and could consider themselves outside contenders for the title. The side had been required to prove their mettle after a disappointing start to their league campaign, but Ferguson said he was not surprised that his side had turned the game around.

'I can believe the run we're on because I know we're capable of this,' he said. 'I don't think anybody in the game would disagree that we could do this kind of run. But we've just got to hope others keep making mistakes to give us a chance. Hopefully we can take our chances and we will see in April.'

But the resurgent Reds had the wind taken out of their sails by Liverpool, who completed a league double with a 1–0 win at Old Trafford. United's FA Cup adventures also fell short as Middlesbrough secured safe passage with a 2–0 victory to stun Ferguson's Reds at the fourth-round stage. Ferguson had reverted to a traditional 4–4–2 thanks to the form of Ole Solskjaer, and the Norwegian repaid the manager's faith by hitting a hat-trick in the 4–0 victory over Bolton at the Reebok, exacting a small amount of revenge for their victory at the Theatre of Dreams.

United stayed in contention with victories over Sunderland and Charlton but dropped points at Derby and showed their vulnerability in early March. Malcolm Christie had put Derby ahead inside six minutes only for Scholes to equalise five minutes before half time. Verón scored on the hour mark to put United ahead, but Christie struck again to share the spoils. In the absence of Roy Keane, Scholes and Verón had taken on the central midfield partnership, with Beckham and Giggs back to their best on the flanks – and Ferguson would have been pleased to see both his attacking midfielders find the back of the net.

Giggs and Beckham, who had been United mainstays during the treble-winning season and beyond, found themselves susceptible to Ferguson's rotation policy in trying to accommodate his wealth of midfield riches. Giggs was benched for the visit of Tottenham to Old Trafford, with Scholes occupying a left-sided position in a fluent United attack which proved too strong for Spurs, as Beckham and van Nistelrooy bagged braces in a 4–0 win.

After Jaap Stam had been sold to Lazio in acrimonious circumstances in the summer, the defence had looked weak, despite the acquisition of veteran French centre back Laurent Blanc. These frailties were brought to light at Upton Park in a scintillating display of attacking football. Beckham, Scholes, Keane and Butt were the chosen midfield combination for the trip to east London but found themselves a goal behind inside ten minutes through Steve Lomas. David Beckham fired a response on 17 minutes, only for Frédi Kanouté to hit back three minutes later. Butt responded on 22 minutes to restore parity as a breathless first half concluded with the teams deadlocked at two apiece.

Scholes fired in a fine goal on 55 to edge United ahead, with Solskjaer making it 4–2 on the hour mark. Jermaine Defoe struck ten minutes from time to set up an uncomfortable climax, but a late Beckham penalty gave United their second 5–3 victory in London that season.

Despite vast improvements, as the season wore on United still could not claim victory over Middlesbrough, who picked up a 1–0 win at Old Trafford, much to the frustration of the United faithful. Defensive frailties came back to haunt the side once again, but, even with van Nistelrooy given a rare rest, United did not struggle for goals. Scholes was moved forward once again in Ferguson's latest reshuffle, but he scored in the ninth minute, only to have his effort cancelled out by Australian Mark Viduka. Solskjaer responded with two goals in as many minutes to put United 3–1 up at half time. Ryan Giggs made it 4–1 early in the second half before goals from Ian Harte and Lee Bowyer, which set up a frantic climax across the Pennines. United held on for another heart-stopping victory.

Juan Verón, having plied his trade in Italy after his move to from South America, was well suited to European competition and reserved many of his finest performances for the Champions League. Ferguson favoured his new formation in Europe after watching his side fail to live up to the standards set in 1999. United's traditional 4–4–2 system was too rigid to trouble fluent European sides.

The quarter-final draw pitted the Reds against group rivals Deportivo on 2 April. The Spanish side had beaten them both home and away earlier in the campaign and the tie offered a great challenge to the much-improved United side. Ferguson opted for Nicky Butt and Roy Keane to anchor the centre of midfield, while Scholes shifted forward alongside van Nistelrooy. This time, United picked up a victory on a European away trip, with first-half goals from Beckham and van Nistelrooy taking United through to the semi-finals of the competition for the first time since Barcelona in 1999.

The season would prove critical for Scholes, with United still in reach of the Champions League and with a World Cup to come in the summer. With the season now reaching the business end, Scholes admitted it was time for a change.

'My form wasn't good enough early on. I hope I can turn that around now', he told the *Manchester Evening News*. 'The position I was being asked to play does actually suit me. But unfortunately it wasn't working for me personally and I don't know why. I wasn't playing well and maybe there was a lack of confidence. I didn't have a good start to the season and it took me a while to get a goal. However, I want to play well in every game now because every match we play from now on is massive.'

Leverkusen had proved a thorn in United's side in recent years but Scholes said United would need to forget about the past and concentrate on the job in hand. 'We haven't got a score to settle but we should have won both matches against them.'

Scholes flirted with suspension, having picked up a series of bookings at the beginning of 2002, and one more against opponents Leicester would see him suspended for the two final Premier League matches, which could have proved critical. Scholes was on immaculate behaviour, however, and United wrapped up a 1–0 win over the Foxes.

With Arsenal showing no signs of slowing down in their quest for the title, United made light work of a potentially tricky match with Chelsea, with a Scholes-inspired side easing to a 3–0 victory. The 27-year-old midfielder struck the crucial first goal to set United on their way to victory. The first leg of the quarter-finals of the Champions League took place at Old Trafford in late May, with United surrendering two away goals in a 2–2 draw – which gave the German side a priceless advantage. United needed to score in the return match if they were to progress, but a 1–1 draw sent them crashing out of the competition, agonisingly close to a place in the final. Ultimately, the giant trophy would be going to Madrid, as a Zidane-inspired side crushed the Germans by three goals to nil.

After the despair of their midweek plight, Manchester United needed to regroup and beat Arsenal in the title decider at Old Trafford on 8 May. Victory for the Gunners would see them crowned champions, while a United win would blow the race wide open again. The day was to belong to Arsène Wenger, however, with Sylvain's Wiltord's solitary goal bringing his side that crowning glory. With victory in the FA Cup, Wenger had steered his side to the double, a worthy reward for a season of hard graft, but United needed to find a position to utilise the best of Paul Scholes if they were to be able to challenge the Gunners for domestic dominance.

Chapter 6

TRAVEL SICKNESS

'He will be the first to admit that last season in spells he did
not play as well as he normally does.'

ERIC HARRISON

Finishing third the previous season meant United had to
negotiate a Champions League qualifier against Zalaegerszeg,
a previously unknown Hungarian side, in order to secure their
place in the lucrative group stages of the competition. Scholes
took no part in the opening game in Hungary, which a sluggish
United lost 1–0, but picked up an injury in the return leg at
Old Trafford. United proved far too strong on home soil and
breezed past their lowly opponents 5–1 on aggregate, with
Scholes bagging the third in a comfortable stroll at the Theatre
of Dreams.

Sir Alex Ferguson was on the verge of a midfield crisis with
Roy Keane's long term knee problems and could ill afford more
problems in the midfield engine room. 'He could be out for two

weeks', Ferguson told Manchester's *Evening News*. 'It is difficult with an ankle and the swelling went up immediately. He went over on it but hopefully it will only be two weeks.'

Scholes played through the pain as United picked up another three points at home to Middlesbrough on 3 September, but was forced to spend much of the month on the sidelines due to the persistent, niggling problem with his knee. Injuries had hampered Scholes's start to the season but he returned with a bang at the end of the month and scored the equaliser against Charlton to set United on their way to a 3–1 victory at The Valley.

'I'm very pleased. It's nice to be playing,' he told MUTV. 'It's not nice sitting on the sidelines watching, and the goal was a bonus for me. The return to fitness has been quite quick. My first goal of the season has come a bit quicker than last season, so, hopefully, I can follow it up with a few more.'

While Scholes may have endured one of his worst seasons in a red shirt during the previous campaign, many felt he had begun to get to grips with the 'problem' role of supporting United's strikers – and in particular the prolific Ruud van Nistelrooy. 'Mentally he didn't come to terms with his role last season,' Ferguson told the *Express*. 'But he has done now – he definitely brings a dimension to our game, which we need.'

The player himself, meanwhile, admitted he was beginning to feel more comfortable in the specialist role carved for him by the Scottish tactician. 'Playing upfront has worked a bit more this season and I've been playing in midfield as well, but as long as I'm in the team it doesn't matter where I play. We're creating chances and, with the players we have, we're capable of scoring.'

United would need to be firing on all cylinders if they were to mount a decent challenge in the Champions League group stages. Eric Harrison, former youth team coach, cast his eye over the fortunes of United's class of '92 ten years on and lavished praise upon Scholes for his adaptability – proving he is irreplaceable for Manchester United.

'Paul is a dream,' he told the *Manchester Evening News*. 'He will be the first to admit that last season in spells he did not play as well as he normally does. He was probably worried about it because it just wasn't there for him. But apparently he has got his head around his 'new' position but it is not a new position for him as far as I can see. He can play here without any question because he is a forward-minded player.'

Fortunately, Ferguson's trial formation when playing in Europe, utilising Scholes and Juan Verón as creative midfield outlets, had begun to pay dividends on the Continent, and they brushed aside Greek champions Panathinaikos with two goals in each half.

Scholes's prayers for more goals this term were soon answered as he bagged a brace in the 3–0 demolition of Everton at Old Trafford. Ahead of his two-goal haul, Scholes sent out a message of intent to title rivals Arsenal, pledging to fight to the death for United's title cause when played in the supporting striker's role.

'It is the perfect position for me,' he told the *Express*. 'Hopefully I can play well there by making goals and trying to score some as well. We are starting to look strong now and we can compete with Arsenal.'

United looked out of sorts on 19 October as they were held to a draw by west Londoners Fulham at Craven Cottage, but returned to form in the midweek Champions League fixture against Panathinaikos. The Greek side are notoriously difficult to beat on home soil, while being hopeless on their travels, and United showed grit and determination to pick up a battling 3–2 win. Once again, Scholes was among the scorers, netting what would prove to be the winner six minutes from time to send Ferguson's men home with an invaluable three points.

After the match Ryan Giggs spoke of his admiration for the flame-haired midfielder, admitting that his ability to find the net from anywhere on the pitch made him a priceless asset. 'Paul's capable is scoring all types of goals,' Giggs said. 'He can score poachers goals; he can hit them superbly from outside the box as well and can score headers. It's a great asset he's got and that's what he's capable of.'

In the build-up to Christmas an off-colour Scholes hit a slump in front of goal, going a month without finding the back of the net. He spelled disaster for United, who also suffered a mid-season blip with a number of high-profile defeats. An under-strength Manchester United – who were already assured a place in the next round of the competition – were humbled 3–0 in a hostile Champions League encounter with Maccabi Haifa in Israel, a result that Scholes confessed was embarrassing for the team.

'You can say we had a weakened side but we still had some quality players on the field and we should have been able to beat a team like Maccabi,' he said. 'We didn't play well enough, it's as simple as that. We have to try to get back to winning ways. We're already through but it would be nice to win the group.'

United edged past Premier League strugglers Leicester and Southampton before the derby game with Manchester City. United were certainly the form team going into the derby, but Scholes was quick to use the old 'form book goes out of the window' cliché when it came to clashes with the blue half of the city.

'We have normally been as good as our form when it came to derbies,' he told the *Manchester Evening News*. 'In my time in the first team, City have never upset the odds but I don't know whether you would class us as the form team going into this one. We may be unbeaten for a while in the league but we have drawn more games then we would have liked, and we are not winning games convincingly like in past years.

'I think it is a must win match for us now. We need the three points to keep us going in the title race. We cannot afford to drop a point at the moment. In terms of that, and also the fact that I think most people, apart from City fans themselves, don't give City fans a chance tomorrow, I think we have far more to lose in this one than City have. It would be far worse for us if we don't get three points. It is an unusual situation for us going into a derby knowing we are not playing as well as we can do.

'In the past we have usually been in decent form. Because of that City may think that if they are ever going to beat us this is the perfect chance, but we are determined that is not going to happen. We want to keep up our good record against them. I hope City fans are confident. Every time there is a derby I hear how City fans are going to win it but in my time we have never lost and invariably we have won. Hopefully their fans will be believing again they can win this one and then we can shut them up!'

As a born-and-bred Mancunian, Scholes could never resist stoking the fires ahead of a derby, admitting it transcended even his own family. 'I have family and friends who are Blues,' he added. 'It is mainly my in-laws who are City fans and they cannot wait to savour a City win again. But I aim to make sure it does not happen.'

Despite Scholes's bravado before the match, he was powerless as City recorded their first victory over United with the Ginger Prince in the side, courtesy of goals from Nicolas Anelka and Shaun Goater. Sadly, it was not the last time Scholes would taste bitter defeat against his rivals, as City would defy the form book and league table to inflict painful victories over United in the years to come – but the first defeat would always sting the most.

United had looked off colour once again and, despite the fact that the season was still in its infancy, there was talk of another trophy-less season at Old Trafford. Ferguson admitted that, while he had assembled a squad of real talent, bruising, combative teams such as Manchester City had the ability to grind out results against his side.

'At the moment we don't have the killer instinct because we are playing the extra pass all the time,' he told the *Sunday Express*. 'We are playing far too much football. If you look at the statistics, we have the best possession of any team in the league. We had 70% of the ball against City – and we still lost. You don't get that much possession against schoolboy teams. What we have to do is mix it up with more effective football and that is something we have already discussed within the club.'

Ferguson continued to vent his frustration at how teams would refuse to attack his side for fear of reprisals on the break. 'Teams don't contest for the ball against us now – they just sit back and leave us with the ball. What has happened is that because we have had such a long run of success, there is not a player in the game who does not know what the strengths of Manchester United are: our style of play, our set pieces, everything. We have no surprises for anyone.'

Ferguson then revealed his thinking behind playing Scholes in a more advanced role – and how he believed it would pay dividends. 'I have played Scholes in attack to try something new, to surprise teams,' he continued. 'Scholes up there has the brain to operate differently. We are trying to utilise that if we can. The problem is that our central midfield is never the same. Sometimes I have to bring him back to that position and then push him up in more important games alongside van Nistelrooy. I will keep doing it as well.'

With that in mind Ferguson was determined to give his fringe players a chance to show they could step in should any of United's 'star' players underperform – and German outfit Bayer Leverkusen certainly posed stiff opposition for the Reds. Ferguson's side needed only a draw to top the group but a goal in each half from Verón and van Nistelrooy sealed United's spot at the top of Champions League Group F. Ferguson hailed Scholes as the best player in the country, insisting that his ability to play in different positions made him an even greater player, not a weakened utility man like the press would have him believe.

'Scholes has been fantastic this season,' the Scot told the *Sunday Mirror*. I think he listened to the critics too much last year when they kept bringing up his role in the team, but that's not a problem now. I simply explained to Paul that great players are capable of playing anywhere. Very few can do that, but Scholes is one of them. That's why, without question, I think that Paul Scholes is the best player in England. He's got the best skills, the best brain. No one can match him.'

While Scholes may have publicly made his peace with the attacking role alongside van Nistelrooy, he believes the added pressure on his shoulders to start delivering goals had an adverse affect on his performances. 'It was quite difficult getting my head round the deep-lying role because all I wanted to do really was just play in midfield the way I had been,' he told the *Manchester Evening News*. 'A different type of pressure came with it because I was suddenly expected to score goals, whereas in my other midfield role goals were more of a bonus. I have scored a few in my career so I was used to some expectancy, but I suddenly felt last year that people's expectations grew. I was expected to go out and score 25–30. But that was never going to happen.

'I think with the chances I get I should be scoring around 15 a season. I scored 18 in my first term but that is a while ago now. I would like to get back to that kind of tally. I've scored five times so far this season so that's a bit better. It has helped me confidence-wise. Last year it was November before I scored my first league goal so that added to the frustration and pressure over the new role.'

While all eyes were focused the previous year on Scholes in his new role, he hoped the expectation had now died down. 'It seemed like everything depended on my success in that role,' he added. 'If United were going to do well in Europe it was down to me handling that role was the way it appeared to be portrayed. But that's not true because we have many special talents in our team. The manager thought it was perfect for me and I thought it would be too.

'But lack of form, lack of goals especially or whatever, it didn't originally work. Pressure doesn't affect me really, it was the frustration of the whole thing more than anything else because I wasn't scoring. I am happier with the role now. It does feel better. I hope it will carry on. And I know there is more to come from me.'

The term 'modern great' circles the sport media too often, but former England legend Sir Tom Finney said Scholes could become a legend in club colours.

'I remember United playing Stan Pearson in the forties and fifties in this role. Then came Dennis Viollet another wonderful player who never gave anything less than 100 per cent. He, too, was an all-action player who went out and gave his all. Nowadays I see Scholes leading the way and carrying on the good work. He, too, is a great little player with a wonderful engine. I like the way he plays the game and he reminds me so much of Alan Ball – always in the thick of the action.

'Stan Pearson and Dennis Viollet were great players in their own right; now Scholes has come to the fore – thriving on taking the game to the opposition. Such players are vital to any team and their consistency speaks for itself – they never ever let you down. They go out and compete for everything. We saw just how committed Scholes is during the Manchester derby – quite a few United players did not play to full potential but he gave it everything. You can always count on these kinds of players.'

United reignited their title charge as the season moved into late November in an eight-goal thriller with Newcastle at Old Trafford. Ruud van Nistelrooy hit a hat-trick for the hosts, but it was Scholes who opened the scoring with a pinpoint drive after 25 minutes. With Juan Verón still jetlagged from international duty, Scholes took the full responsibility of marshalling the Manchester United engine room and proved he could still be a threat in the middle of the park with his well-taken goal.

Ole Solskjaer netted United's fifth on 55 minutes, but Craig Bellamy's 75th-minute goal was not enough to save the Magpies from a 5–3 defeat. The game sparked an upturn in fortunes for United, who were finally able to string together a run of victories to haul themselves back into contention at the top of the league. Arsenal were still the runaway leaders but United were slowly chipping away at the lead.

Victory in Switzerland over Basle in the Champions League was followed by wins over Liverpool and Burnley ahead of the make-or-break match with Arsenal at Old Trafford. In the corresponding fixture the previous season, Arsenal had strolled past their hosts to capture the title but were faced with a rejuvenated and in-form Manchester United – and the Gunners simply could not cope. Ferguson predictably moved Scholes upfront against one of the Premier League's stronger sides, with Juan Verón given his chance in the centre of midfield despite nagging doubts over his ability to handle the pace of the Premier League – and, indeed, it was the Argentine who gave United the lead after 22 minutes.

The Old Trafford midfield was well marshalled by Phil Neville, who outplayed Arsenal's much-lauded captain, Patrick Vieira, in a man-of-the-match performance. Scholes made the points safe in emphatic style after the interval, turning inside a static Martin Keown to lash home United's second – and to send out a message of intent to their title rivals.

Buoyed by their victory over Wenger's side, United made it six wins out of six in the Champions League by seeing off Deportivo la Coruña, emphatically booking their place in the next round of Europe's premier club competition. Victory over Chelsea on 17 December continued United's fine streak, but a Christmas wobble would once again come back to haunt the Reds. A single goal from Gary Flitcroft five days later ended the Reds' winning run, and a Boxing Day clash with Middlesbrough went the way of the Teessiders, who breezed to a 3–1 win.

In the final game of 2002, United strolled past Birmingham with a 2–0 win to see off the year with a win.

New Year's Day 2003, brought a clash with Sunderland at Old Trafford and Paul Scholes netted the first in an astonishing run of goals that would eventually power United towards the title.

The Black Cats had taken an early lead due to an own goal from Verón and looked to be heading to defeat before David Beckham struck in the 81st minute. Scholes then struck a priceless winner to give United all three points at Old Trafford. Beckham admitted that United were minutes away from surrendering the title – and hailed the win as one of the most important of the season.

'It was a vital match for us to win,' he told the *Manchester Evening News*. 'We all knew that we couldn't afford to draw against Sunderland, let alone lose. We showed a lot of character and created a host of chances but I must admit that when Scholes's shot hit both posts and bounced back to their keeper, you started to wonder if it was going to be one of those days.'

Having picked up the scent of goal, Scholes was now ready to take the domestic competitions by storm, and was on the scoresheet again in the FA Cup third-round win over Portsmouth. Two penalties from van Nistelrooy had put United in charge before Scholes struck, again in the dying moments, to round off a convincing 4–1 win over the south coast club. United's second string had fought their way to the semi-finals of the League Cup but were provided with tough opposition in the form of Blackburn Rovers.

Ferguson ditched his tried-and-tested formula of blooding young players and opted for a full-strength side to face their Lancashire rivals. Scholes struck his third in three games to give United the lead on the hour mark, only for James McEveley to level three minutes later to claim a draw. United were now rampant in the league and Scholes netted his fourth goal in the

3-1 win over West Brom at the Hawthorns. Former swashbuckling United captain Bryan Robson believed Scholes would soon top his season best tally of 14 goals if he continued his current glut in front of goal.

'I can certainly see Paul getting 20 this season', he told the *Manchester Evening News.* 'He's a fantastic striker of a ball and as good as I have ever seen. He hits a football like the world's best golfers strike through with their shots. It's a fantastic technique. Not only that but he has this special knack of timing runs into the danger area. Defenders can often learn to read a striker's run or positioning but picking up a midfielder who steals in from deep is the most difficult marking job for defenders to cope with.

'Paul gets double figures most seasons but now I think he is definitely capable of getting 20 to his name. For my money he has been United's best player this season by a million miles. It will take something to dislodge him as the Reds' player of the season. He has unquestionably been the most consistent performer. He's had no little blips at all, even during the spell when United were having a tough time he kept his form.

'People say that international players suffer in a post-World Cup season. They reckon the tiredness catches up with you having played in the summer but Scholes had a good World Cup for England in Japan and has come back this term stronger and better. This season he is as good as I have ever seen him.'

Robson, who marshalled United's midfield throughout the late 1980s and early 1990s, agreed that Scholes had grown into the role carved out for him by Sir Alex Ferguson.

'No matter how much you think a player may be suited to a certain task it can take a while to adapt,' he continued. 'It doesn't matter how highly you are rated – even the best players can't always take to things straight away. I think that's what you had last season with Paul. But now he's playing the role as well as anyone I know. Zinédine Zidane at Real Madrid operates in a similar way, as does Dennis Bergkamp at Arsenal. However, through injuries and selection they've not been doing it to Paul's standards week in, week out.

'It's an illustrious pair to be compared with but that is the heights Paul Scholes has taken his game to. I've talked about his goalscoring but he is also a very intelligent player whose vision is outstanding. If you give Scholesy three options for a pass and he'll always pick the correct one. He has a terrific football brain. He's maturing as a person and a player.'

Scholes continued his charge towards the 20-goal target by steering United to victory over Chelsea in their next game, making it five goals in five games since the start of the year. Despite his success, Scholes remained typically modest when asked about his current form. 'A bit of luck's helped me,' he told MUTV. 'Things like my goal against West Brom have been going in, whereas last year they'd be hitting the post or would have gone wide. The goal against Blackburn was lucky as well. Things seem to be falling in the right place for me and I'm getting on the end of things better than last year.'

It has been a trait of Manchester United Football Club to leave it late to snatch the points, and the same was true of the meeting with the west Londoners. After falling behind to Eidur

Gudjohnsen's goal, Scholes restored parity before a goal at the death by Uruguayan striker Diego Forlán, capping another fantastic comeback by the Reds – who were beginning to show the never-say-die attitude that had steered them to treble success in 1999.

'Goal-wise I don't think I have ever seen him have a better season. Twelve goals at this stage of the season is fantastic,' Ferguson told the *Manchester Evening News*.

'As well as the goals, Scholesy is in great form,' he added. 'What he is showing now is great maturity. It doesn't matter where I ask him to play, like midfield on Saturday in the second half, even sometimes towards the left of midfield, the right side, or up front, he copes with it and does a great job. He is wiser and more mature. He is using his experience and is not fazed by anything and that's because he is a footballer. He is a terrific player and can play any position. Scholesy could even play in goal! I'm serious. He used to do that in training when we were having kick-ins. If you needed to put someone in goal in an emergency you wouldn't worry about Scholesy. He'd love it. He can play anywhere. He might not be that big for the crosses but he'd be brave enough to have a go for them.

'He's always been a great player. What he had at 13 and 14 he's never lost. That vision and his good feet have always been with him. He is two short of his best return of 14 goals in a season and with three months to go, and in this form, you'd have to say it's going to be his best year, surely.'

But, while Scholes may have adapted to his new role with ease this term, Ferguson believed the press were behind his slump during the previous one. 'I think he read the papers too much last year,' Fergie said. 'He listened to what they were saying about the role too much and put a question mark in his head. He was ideal to play the role.'

The papers were now full of Scholes's startling run of form, and he added a brace in the second leg of the League Cup semi-final to book United a place in the Cardiff showpiece. After falling behind early on, Scholes struck twice before the interval before a late van Nistelrooy penalty. Seven goals in six games is a magnificent return for even the most deadly of strikers, but, for a midfielder playing off the prolific Ruud van Nistelrooy, Scholes had proved himself as the top midfielder in the league.

With Scholes firing on all cylinders, United had stormed back into contention at the top of the league – and his performances were earning high praise from across British football. Former England midfielder Malcolm Macdonald, who worked tirelessly in the Three Lions' midfield engine room, compared Scholes to World Cup winning midfielder Alan Ball.

'Scholes is a brilliant little player whose skill and play reminds me so much of Bally,' he said. 'Manchester United are at their best when Scholes is at his most effective. I think he is a fantastic footballer. Alan Ball was a great player – he could create chances, he had great vision and he could score goals – so can Scholes. Alan also had a wonderful engine – he was everywhere on a field and this is also seen in Paul's make-up – he too is so talented.'

Scholes had been given his first chance in a United shirt in the

League Cup and his brace had helped seal a dream final against Liverpool in a competition that rarely concerned the Premier League's upper echelons. But a Lancashire–Merseyside derby was sure to get pulses racing and reignite interest in the competition. 'Liverpool–Manchester United games are fantastic,' Ferguson said. 'It doesn't matter if you were playing tiddlywinks it will be fantastically competitive.'

First there was a run of league matches that would help shape United's league season. United hit six past a hapless West Ham on 26 January but, amazingly, Scholes was not on the scoresheet, the first time he had drawn a blank in 2003. Comfortable wins over Southampton and Birmingham followed as United gathered pace going into February. Their charge faltered, however, in the Manchester derby, as City fought back to claim a point, with Shaun Goater once again the scourge of the United defence, finding the back of the net with five minutes remaining to earn a point for the Blues.

At the start of February Scholes was rewarded with the Player of the Month award, incredibly the first time he had ever picked up the trophy, despite being a Manchester United mainstay for the best part of a decade.

'I'm delighted to win the Barclaycard Player of the Month for the first time,' Scholes said. 'I'm very pleased with my form of late, and hoping I can help United keep the pressure on Arsenal at the top of the league.'

The awards panel, meanwhile, accepted that it was difficult to believe Scholes had never previously been given the honour. It said in the announcement,

His pace, eye for goal and intelligence in midfield have been central to United's recent improvement in form. He will be a key player as United try to win the Barclaycard Premiership. Eight league goals this season go some way to explain why this diminutive Mancunian is respected as one of the best players in the world at present.

Despite his new accolade, Scholes was unable to fire United to derby glory. While defeat to United's local rivals may have hurt him deeply, a crushing FA Cup defeat at the hands of Arsenal destroyed United's four-fronted assault on domestic and European competitions. The game against the Gunners was an ill-tempered one, with both sides releasing pent-up frustrations from a long and hard title scrap. A goal in each half from Edu and Sylvain Wiltord settled the fifth-round tie for Wenger's men – and left United battered and bruised ahead of a Champions League clash with Juventus in the second-group stage of the competition.

United hosted the first clash with the Turin giants on 19 February. While rumours of a flu bug circulated around the Old Lady dressing room, United took full advantage and claimed a major scalp in their quest for European glory with a 2–1 win at Old Trafford – with a rare goal from Wes Brown setting the Reds on their way to victory. Injury would rule Scholes out of the return match at the Della Alpi, with a groin problem forcing him out of the next league match at Bolton's Reebok stadium also. While the Juventus side boasted a wealth of European experience, Ferguson was keen to stress that his own side had

European know-how – with a strong group of players who could lead United to more success in the competition.

Scholes had amassed 66 appearances in the Champions League, while fellow youth team graduates David Beckham, Gary Neville and Ryan Giggs had 75, 73 and 66 respectively. 'Continuity is vital in terms of getting a rounded experience,' the United manager told the Associated Press news agency. 'Quite a few of the lads have stayed the trip with us and that is testimony to their consistency, which is vital at our club. We need people who are consistent. Through that consistency you see the results in Europe are consistent, particularly in the last two years.

'The beauty is keeping them for a long time together. The core of them has played European football since the Champions League started. It is a long period to keep your team together but it has its dividends. After winning the cup in 1999, teams planned against us the following season,' he adds. 'We kept getting caught on the counter-attack, even away from home against the likes of Anderlecht and PSV Eindhoven, which if you are supposed to garner experience that shouldn't happen. Knowing how to play in Europe has taken time. They know the tactical part much, much better now. They know tactics have a part to play. Sometimes in England you play to the crowd.

'Juventus have great experience but they still have a willingness to play and that's why I am proud of my own players. Some of my players have had nine years at the top end of the game battling for championships and in European football, but they still have a good attitude to playing.'

As if to prove a point, United swept to victory in Turin, proving they could win on the road at one of Europe's toughest grounds, and, buoyed by their victory over the group favourites, could look forward to a place in the quarter-finals.

Scholes returned in early march for the crunch match with Liverpool at Cardiff's Millennium Stadium as the two Northwest giants contested the Worthington Cup final – the first piece of silverware on offer in the domestic calendar. A goal in each half from Steven Gerrard and Michael Owen settled a tepid final in the Welsh capital – and for Manchester United there were bigger fish to fry.

By March United were nine points behind Arsenal, who looked to have one hand on the Premier League trophy, despite the best efforts of Scholes and his United teammates. The side never stopped battling, fuelled by a desire to deny Arsène Wenger the glory of retaining the title. Victories over Leeds, Aston Villa and Fulham kept United in touch with the Gunners, who had begun to show chinks in their usually impregnable armour. United had breezed through their Champions League group, thanks to the two victories over Juventus, and were drawn against Spanish giants Real Madrid in the quarter-finals – a mouthwatering tie that loomed in April.

The weekend before the match with Los Merengues, United had the chance for revenge against Liverpool, with the three points on offer more valuable to their cause than the Worthington Cup. A Ruud van Nistelrooy brace, along with goals from Ryan Giggs and Ole Solskjaer, gave United a crushing victory over the Merseysiders and plenty of confidence going into the business end of the season. Ferguson's side had hacked away at Arsenal's lead and were fighting on two fronts, both home and abroad, for the two trophies most dear to them.

The Santiago Bernabéu stadium, a concrete mass with three vast tiers housing fanatical Madridistas, has been the scene for many of Europe's greatest football matches. Real Madrid are perhaps the only side who can rival United for history in European football, having lifted the trophy more times than any other side. In a team boasting Luís Figo, Zinédine Zidane, Raul and Ronaldo, they proved a class apart on the night and thoroughly outplayed the Reds for large periods, backed by close to 90,000 fans.

Goals from Figo and Raul had put Madrid 3–0 up before van Nistelrooy reduced the deficit on 52 minutes and, despite battling hard, a 3–1 scoreline was a fair reflection of the play. With a seemingly limitless budget, Real had assembled one of the finest squads of the past ten years, and United defender Gary Neville admitted that their football was awe-inspiring.

'It was breathtaking in the first half,' he said. 'People will say we paid them too much respect and we were nervous but sometimes it's not about that. It wasn't anything to do with those things. Sometimes you do have to admire it. They're capable of wonderful football. They were like the Harlem Globetrotters in the first half at times and it looked like we were getting a bit of a doing. We just didn't get near them in the first half and it was a big problem for us and disappointing. We were too defensive and were better when we went at them in the second half.'

United responded by thrashing Newcastle 6–2 at Old

Trafford, with Scholes banging in a lethal hat-trick to punish the hapless Magpies.

After his hat-trick success, Scholes argued that United were coming into form at the perfect moment. 'You'd like to think the momentum is bubbling just at the right time,' he told the *Manchester Evening News.* We've had two great wins and now hopefully we can carry it on at Highbury. It is always nice to score goals and I haven't scored for a couple of months. One, two or three it doesn't matter; it is just great to score.

'Every goal was worked well and I was happy to be on the end of a few. I hope to add to that now and score some more. It was very enjoyable. Coming off a tough game I think we'd have gone for a 1–0 win but, 4–1 up at half time and playing really well, we wanted to score more. Every player looked like they could score a goal and we had so many chances we could have had eight or nine.

'It was a great performance. I don't think we will play much better than that again and I don't think we have played much better than that before. Everyone is happy. You can't not be after the last couple of weeks although we were disappointed in Europe. The two League games have been great for us. It is a great boost going to Highbury three points ahead.'

Alex Ferguson admitted he would be looking to Scholes to continue his scoring form, having got over his lean patch in front of goal. 'Paul's hat-trick has come at a great time for us. He was the happiest man in the dressing room on Saturday night,' Fergie told *MEN Sport* (the *Manchester Evening News*'s sports supplement). 'It will be onwards and forwards as far as he is concerned. That's the way Scholesy will be looking at it. We don't see him as a goalscorer first and foremost because he also has a fantastic football brain. But I think he is recognised as a goalscorer by some people and I know he loves scoring himself.

'So when you go 13 games without a goal then it starts to affect you. You begin to wonder where your next goal is coming from. Paul had that marvellous run of goals in January when he scored seven in six successive matches. Then he had a chest infection going into the FA Cup match against West Ham. He struggled with it all week and so I had to leave him out of the Southampton match.

'Unfortunately, it got in the way of his scoring run. It stopped him in his tracks and he couldn't get going again in front of goal. But it was a marvellous hat-trick at Newcastle and it couldn't have been better timed.'

United had finally overthrown Arsenal at the top of the table and the next match at Highbury was being touted as a possible title decider. Two goals from Thierry Henry were cancelled out by Ryan Giggs and Ruud van Nistelrooy as the two title hopefuls played out an entertaining 2-2 draw – and Arsenal's failure to pick up three points all but ended their title challenge, with the wind well and truly in United's sails. And they kept the momentum with a 3-1 win over Blackburn, with Scholes netting a brace, including his hundredth goal in United colours. A goal century in the famous Red jersey marked a magnificent milestone for Scholes – who joined an elite group of players to surpass that total – made all the more impressive by his playing in midfield.

'It is great to score 100 goals for United and I hope there are more to come from me,' Scholes told the *Manchester Evening News*. 'I have enjoyed scoring goals this season and have more than I have ever got in the past, so hopefully I can score some more. I am just enjoying it at the moment.'

Scholes, despite hitting a rich vein of form, was suspended for the return leg with Real Madrid, and would miss one of the most dramatic European nights Old Trafford had ever witnessed. United would eventually take the match 4–3, but a sumptuous hat-trick by Ronaldo meant they could not overturn the two-goal deficit from the first game, and crashed out 6–5 on aggregate.

Roy Keane, typically honest, admits he feared that United's glory days in Europe were over after the agonising defeat. 'I probably feel worse this time than I did against Bayer Leverkusen last year,' he said after the game. 'Every year you think you have a good chance of winning the competition but the seasons keep going by and we don't do it. Football's all about winning and losing is something I find hard to accept. The game against Real was probably enjoyable for the fans but that's a small consolation.

'I've said many times that getting to the quarter-finals is one thing. Once you're there you have to get over the final hurdle, and we don't seem able to do it. I'm not sure why we're not consistently getting beyond this stage. Maybe it's just that we're not good enough.'

So, with the Champions League now out of their grasp yet again, United were made to settle for the Premier League. While this may seem ample achievement for Liverpool or Arsenal, United were striving for more, and would need something special if they were to consider themselves the greatest club in the world. Domestic dominance was not enough, but three wins over Tottenham, Charlton and Everton gave Manchester United their eighth league title in 11 years.

Chapter 7

THE GOLDEN GENERATION DISBAND

'I never thought when David Beckham left that one day it could be me. The only thing on your mind is keeping your place in the team. If you are not playing well enough, then maybe you will get sold.'

PAUL SCHOLES

Over the summer Real Madrid courted David Beckham in the hope of luring the now-global superstar to the Spanish capital. Sir Alex Ferguson had become increasingly frustrated at the lifestyle the England captain led, and Los Merengues completed a deal in the region of £23 million. Beckham's departure broke up the legendary class of '92 and Scholes was desperate to avoid any further upheaval in the side.

'It is part of football that people leave clubs and go somewhere else. We are used to the odd big player leaving us now and then,' he told the *Manchester Evening News*. 'I don't feel more vulnerable now than I did before. You always know as a footballer that there is a chance that you could be playing for somebody

131

else at any time. You hope when you are at United that that won't happen. You just hope it doesn't happen to yourself.'

Scholes remarked that it was unique to have so many players stay with the same club for such a long period of time, but the honeymoon must end eventually. 'I never thought when David Beckham left that one day it could be me. The only thing on your mind is keeping your place in the team. If you are not playing well enough, then maybe you will get sold. But as long as you stay in the team you should be alright. You never know about the future,' he continued.

'Circumstances change. If you can't get in the team all you want to do is play football and if you find yourself sub every week or not in the side you don't want to be hanging about. But like I have said a hundred times, I want to stay. It would be ideal to stay at United for the rest of my life but ideal things don't always happen.'

Scholes's sparkling form the previous season, reaching the 20-goal mark from midfield, won him widespread acclaim and all but guaranteed a starting place in Ferguson's starting line-up for the new season. 'Goals-wise I have not had a better season than last year,' he added. 'Whether it was my best otherwise, I don't know. I have no idea why the goals have started coming. Every season I get chances but I took most of them last time. In the past I have missed them – that is the major difference. People will probably be expecting me to do that again now but while I want to make goals as well, I don't mind being judged on my goals. I enjoy scoring goals and it is the most important part of any game so it is nice to contribute.'

There was to be more upheaval in the middle of the Manchester United midfield, with Juan Verón ending an inauspicious spell at Old Trafford by signing for Chelsea in a cut-price £15 million deal. Paris St Germain's Brazilian wizard Ronaldinho was seen as the ideal replacement for David Beckham, but he opted to join Barcelona. American goalkeeper Tim Howard joined as cover for Fabian Barthez, while David Bellion and Eric Djemba-Djemba inked deals at Old Trafford to bolster the squad, aiming for their ninth Premier League title.

United and Arsenal contested the Charity Shield at the Millennium Stadium, with little to choose between the two sides but with United eventually bettering their north London rivals in a penalty shoot-out. Scholes started on the left flank against the Gunners and, despite a magnificent display in an unfavourable position, many felt he was being wasted out wide. Former United manager Ron Atkinson, in a column in the *Manchester Evening News*, said Scholes must be brought back into the centre if Old Trafford was to see the best of him. He wrote,

Scholes didn't have a shot or even get into a position to have a shot from the left against Arsenal. Although he showed what a great all-round game he has got with his display there before he moved inside. The downside of playing Scholes in that position is that he gets into the box far less than when he is operating off the front and for me that is a waste because he is the best goal-scoring midfielder in Europe. I feel he should be used in a more orthodox position behind van Nistelrooy. He can still get

*involved in all the build up play but is then much more able
to get into the box and finish things. He and van Nistelrooy
can both make tracks for the penalty area and that is a
sight no opposition manager wants to see.*

United hosted Northwest rivals Bolton Wanderers at Old
Trafford as their title defence kicked off in style. A Ryan Giggs
brace was added to by Scholes on 77 minutes, before van
Nistelrooy wrapped up a 4–0 win three minutes from time. A
young Cristiano Ronaldo made his debut as a second-half
substitute for Nicky Butt. The Portuguese winger had been
captured from Sporting Lisbon for £12 million and his emerging
talent on either flank would allow Scholes to move back inside
to a more central position.

Ferguson had spent big on foreign stars in recent years, hoping
to bolster his side with the cream of world football's crop, but
Nobby Stiles, a former United great, believed Scholes and his
former youth-team compatriots would fight off any challenge to
their places.

'Being Mancunians has helped them,' he told the *Evening
News.* 'They have pride in it, as players like myself and Brian Kidd
had. Scholesy is a big favourite – there is no edge to him and you
never see him in the papers. He could play in any position: full
back, goalkeeper, anything – because he has a great knowledge
of the game and clearly he loves it.'

Scholes continued his flying start to the season with the
second goal as United came from behind to beat Newcastle at St
James' Park. Ferguson was sent to the stands but, led by

inspirational captain Roy Keane, United fought back from Alan Shearer's first-half strike to take all three points. Victories over Wolves and Leicester followed before a surprise defeat in the Champions League opener to Stuttgart in southern Germany.

Scholes bagged his third of the season in early October as United returned to form with a 3–0 demolition of Birmingham at Old Trafford. Before the game Birmingham boss Steve Bruce, a former United skipper, spoke of his fear at the return to form of Scholes. 'It is a massive challenge going to United because they are simply the best team in the country,' he told the *Manchester Evening News*. 'And to cap it all, Scholesy got himself fit just at the wrong time for us. He is the best player in Britain in my opinion and he has to get himself fit just before we are due to play at Old Trafford!

'I cannot pay Paul a bigger compliment than to say that he is the most complete footballer in the country. The best bar none. United are a fantastic team with some truly great players bit, for me, Scholes is the one who sets the standards at Old Trafford.'

Bruce had every reason to feel concerned: Van Nistelrooy broke the deadlock with a first-half penalty before Scholes doubled the advantage on the hour mark. Ryan Giggs made the points safe ten minutes from time as United continued their excellent start to the domestic campaign.

Scholes took his now customary position behind van Nistelrooy for the trip across the Pennines to face Leeds United – which was decided by a solitary Roy Keane strike on 81 minutes.

The Champions League threw up an intriguing home nations derby as United took on Glasgow stalwarts Rangers at Ibrox.

Scholes had enjoyed success north of the border with the national side on the way to the Euro 2000 finals, and he admitted that United's mantle of favourites could come back to haunt them, as it nearly did England.

'It wasn't the Hampden atmosphere that was the worry up there, that wasn't actually that bad,' he told the *Manchester Evening News*. 'But England were expected to walk the tie and that is what built up the pressure on us. That is not the same kind of pressure we are under this time with United at Ibrox. Rangers have a much better team than Scotland had. They have a lot of quality players. They are nearer to us in quality than Scotland were to England in '99.

'So it is a different situation we are going into. The pressure for this one comes because of our defeat in the group against Stuttgart in Germany last time out. If we lose at Ibrox it will put us in a really awkward position and it will be tough to get out of it. It is important we get something in Scotland. Not qualifying is not something we want to think about. We want to go all the way but I think it is down to three teams in this group: us, Rangers and Stuttgart.

'Since the treble season in '99 when we had Barcelona, Bayern Munich and Brøndby in our group we have always been quite lucky with our group draws in Europe.'

A rare Phil Neville goal in the fifth minute gave United a hard-fought win against a Rangers side boasting quality in Mikel Arteta, Peter Løvenkrands and Shota Arveladze.

Scholes was relegated to the bench for the visit of Fulham to Old Trafford amid injury worries, but was brought into the action as a substitute for Cristiano Ronaldo on 69 minutes with the west London side already 2–1 ahead. Japan's Junichi Inamoto, formerly of Arsenal, scored ten minutes from time to secure a shock victory for the Cottagers. After the game a United spokesman confirmed that Scholes would face a spell on the sidelines due to a niggling injury: 'Paul Scholes's groin problem has re-occurred and he has had to have surgery to both groins. He is likely to be out for three to four weeks.'

Scholes's fine form over the previous twelve months was rewarded with a nomination for the European Footballer of the Year award alongside teammate Ruud van Nistelrooy in the 50-strong group of nominees. Scholes had won plenty of plaudits for his displays, including praise from the tenacious Dutch midfielder Edgar Davids, and Sir Alex Ferguson admits he is not surprised by the praise. 'I wouldn't disagree with him,' he told the *Manchester Evening News*. Every time you hear an opponent speaking about Manchester United – and quite a lot of them do that – they always seem to refer to Scholes's ability.

'When you have scored the goals he has scored as a midfield player – and he has been doing it for years – he obviously has talent. He scored 20 for us last years and it's over 100 for the club in total, that's amazing. We miss Paul's goals and his threat of goals. He has the subtlety to play in tight areas of the game, playing off the front, or as a midfield player. You know that he is such a clever player, at some point he is going to arrive in the box and get you goals. Not being interested in the limelight is what makes Paul such a special person.'

Scholes made his return in early December as a substitute for

Ryan Giggs on the hour mark – with United recording a 4–0 win over the Midlanders. Brazilian midfielder Kléberson, who was tipped for big things after his performances in the 2002 World Cup, had failed to set Old Trafford alight with his displays, but Scholes said he was impressed with the playmaker as an attacking force.

'Most people know him as a central midfielder so they were surprised to see him playing in that role,' he told the *Manchester Evening News*. 'He was fantastic; a lot of one-touch stuff and the ball always seemed to stick. He was looking to play one-twos with Ryan, turning on the ball a lot and getting shots in, which is important in that position. The centre-halves don't know whether to come out to him, and the midfielders don't know whether to come back. It's all about your movement, being able to take the ball and getting shots in.'

While United were looking strong in attack, Scholes praised the United rearguard after a difficult few seasons. 'A couple of seasons ago we were making a lot of mistakes and ending up having to score four or five goals just to win a game,' he continued. 'But eventually those mistakes catch up with you. As long as we are winning I don't really care how well we are playing. We will take three points over a great performance any day.'

Scholes was restored to the starting line-up for the visit of Stuttgart to Old Trafford and instantly reminded the United faithful what they had been missing. The midfielder was instrumental in the 2–0 dismantling of the Germans.

Next up for United was the visit of Manchester City to the

Above: Challenging for the ball during United's 1-1 draw with Porto in the 2004 Champions League.

Below: In the thick of it during England's dramatic Euro 2004 game against France. Despite a solid performance from Scholes, England lost 2-1 thanks to a last-gasp French penalty.

Above: Scholes celebrates his goal as England beat Croatia 4-2 to secure their place in the Euro 2004 quarter-finals.

Below: In training with the England team during Euro 2004.

Above: Scholes celebrates United's 4-1 victory over Newcastle United, sending them into the 2005 FA Cup final.

Below left: In action against AC Milan in the 2005 Champions League – United won this match 1-0.

Below right: Sadly the 2005 FA Cup final did not live up to expectations, with Arsenal winning the trophy on penalties after a 0-0 draw. Scholes was the only United player to miss a penalty in the shoot-out.

Above left: After a disappointing 2004/5 campaign, which saw United finish without any trophies for only the fourth time in 17 seasons, they had to take part in Champions League qualifying. Here, Scholes is pictured in the third round against Debreceni.

Above right: Having made it through to the Champions League proper, Scholes comes under attack in United's game against Lille in October 2005.

Bottom: Winning the ball against Benfica in 2006.

Above left: Scholes was instrumental in United's 3-2 victory over AC Milan in the first leg of their 2007 Champions League semi-final. Unfortunately, Milan won the second leg 3-0 to progress to the final.

Above right: Scholes in action in the 2007/08 Champions League against Roma.

Below left: Taking the captain's armband for a pre-season friendly in 2007.

Below right: Controlling the ball against Portsmouth in the 2008 FA Cup quarter-finals. Portsmouth pulled off a shock 1-0 win over United and went on to lift the trophy.

Above: Scholes shows his delight at his incredible goal against Barcelona in the 2008 Champions League semi-final second leg, which sent United into the final.

Below: The United players celebrate their victory over Barcelona.

Ferguson, meanwhile, leapt to Scholes's defence in the wake of public criticism. 'I'm not worried – he is only 29 for God's sake,' the Scot said. 'He has got plenty of time ahead of him. He's still as important for us as he's ever been.'

United produced some of their best football of the season to see off Sparta Prague at Old Trafford comfortably, but were unable to find a way past a stubborn Manchester City four days later. A comfortable 3-1 win over Newcastle followed before Scholes finally broke his duck, and bagged his first United goal in eight months. Scholes, who had turned thirty earlier in the month, scored the second in a 2-0 win over Charlton at Old Trafford. The game had special significance for Scholes, who was playing in his 300th Premier League match, in front of his home fans, and he admitted the goal was long overdue.

'The chances have been coming in the last couple of weeks and today the goal came,' he told the *Manchester Evening News*. 'I have been trying as hard as ever to score but for one reason or another it hasn't happened until now. Now I want to go on and get more. We are showing signs we are coming back and creating chances – hopefully we can all go on and score a lot more goals. We have maybe six players capable of scoring goals. It is frustrating not doing it but now we can go on from here.'

Scholes said he was irked by Charlton's negative approach, but conceded it was the way many teams set their stall out at Old Trafford. 'They played like most teams down here – they flooded the midfield and didn't think about scoring a goal,' he continued. 'But it is up to us to break them down.'

United had begun to get their season back on track and turned over Lyon 2–1 at Old Trafford in Ferguson's 1,000th game at the helm of Manchester United. There was an electric atmosphere at Old Trafford in celebration of the Scot and Scholes remarked that it was in European competition that United – and Ferguson – still had a point to prove.

'I am as hungry and enthusiastic as I have ever been,' he told the *Express*. I might have turned 30 but I don't feel any different. I still enjoy training every day and playing – the hunger is definitely still there to win things. It is very important to win the European Cup again, not just for me personally but for the club.

'We want to win it every year although we know that is not realistic. We always try to go as far as we can in the competition and hopefully one day we will win it again. We haven't always had the best of luck.'

However, it was against West Brom that Scholes would cement his return to goalscoring form. Former United skipper Bryan Robson watched in horror as the United midfielder tore into his West Bromwich Albion side – and left them marooned at the bottom of the Premier League.

'Scholes had quite a few niggly injuries at the start of the season and missing games can sometimes take the edge off players,' said the former Old Trafford idol. 'But now he's played in quite a few consecutive games and he looks that little bit sharper. But when United play these kinds of attacking players, whichever midfielders and forwards he puts on the pitch, they're all a threat.'

Scholes netted either side of a Ruud van Nistelrooy strike to secure a 3–0 win over the Baggies, and continue United's good run of form.

'A lot of people have spells when they can't score a goal and can't do anything right, but when they hit one they seem to come in bundles,' he told the *Manchester Evening News*. Hopefully I can get a few more now – something like my last run would be nice again. But so long as the team are winning is doesn't matter who is scoring. However, getting back scoring does help with your confidence.'

While a productive month had seen United perform at something like their best, Scholes admitted that it would take something remarkable to dislodge Arsenal and Chelsea.

'We know we have put ourselves in a great position but now we need to win our games and we have to follow this up,' he continued. 'You have to do it a game at a time but we are capable of winning every game and if we want to win the league we have to more or less do that.'

Scholes made it three goals in two games as he broke the deadlock in a 3–0 win over Southampton at Old Trafford, with all the goals coming in the second half. Ahead of the busy Christmas period United carried out a 5–2 demolition of Crystal Palace at Old Trafford, with Scholes bagging a brace as he began to show the kind of consistency in front of goal that had been lacking in the early stages of the season. The midfielder broke the deadlock in the 22nd minute and added a second, United's fourth, shortly after half time before John O'Shea's 90th-minute strike, which completed the rout.

The match, however, was soured by an injury to Ruud van

Nistelrooy that saw the Dutch hitman miss one of the most crucial periods of the season. Ferguson, meanwhile, remained confident the club could maintain their title charge in the absence of their prolific striker.

'I am not happy about not having Ruud, but it doesn't distress me in any way,' he told the *Manchester Evening News*. 'I am satisfied we have the players to compensate. I have Alan Smith and the options of David Bellion, Wayne Rooney, Ryan Giggs and Paul Scholes. They can all play as strikers. There is a far better goal threat about us now – it looks like we can score goals again and our making of chances is good.

'I think someone will take a hiding from us this season,' he continued. 'I think two or three teams will. If we had put our foot down against Palace, we could have scored a lot more. In terms of goals, Scholes has been a real bonus,' he concluded.

Scholes scored a last-minute goal against Bolton to secure a 2–0 win on Boxing Day, while victories over Aston Villa and Middlesbrough took United into 2005 on the crest of a wave. A 0–0 draw with Tottenham Hotspur halted the recharge, but despite taking maximum points over the Christmas period, United had been unable to make up any ground on the league leaders.

'It is a bit frustrating we are still nine points behind Chelsea,' he told the *Manchester Evening News*. 'We thought if we won all our games over the Christmas period, we could chip away at their lead a little bit but it has not been the case. There are still plenty of games to go but I think we will accept it is going to be difficult to pull Chelsea back. The only thing we can do is look after our own results. Confidence is pretty high and if we keep plugging away, hopefully they will slip up.'

United were handed a favourable tie in the first round of the FA Cup in the form of Exeter City, who were delighted to make the trip to Old Trafford for a once-in-a-lifetime opportunity. Scholes was one of few United first-team players to make an appearance, but United's second string were unable to break down the Conference side, who clung on for a famous draw at the Theatre of Dreams. United had been going well in the League Cup and faced Chelsea in the semi-final. The competition was not the sum of either side's ambition, but Scholes was given a starting berth, with the final only two games away. However, the match ended in a goalless draw at Stamford Bridge, with neither side able to force a breakthrough in a tentative ninety minutes. United bounced back by completing a league double over Liverpool courtesy of Wayne Rooney's first-half strike.

United deployed their big guns at Exeter's St James' Park to seal safe passage to the fourth round of the FA Cup. Scholes then bagged the third in a 3-1 win over Villa to complete a morale-boosting victory. Scholes had hoped victory in the semi-final second leg against Chelsea could trigger an end of season wobble for the west London side.

'One bad result and it could all change,' he told the *Mirror*. 'It is not nice to lose games; they haven't had that feeling for a while. You never know how it might affect them. They have plenty of points in hand and we need them to slip up. But if we beat them in the Carling Cup they could start dropping a few points in the league as well.'

Scholes was to be found wanting, however, as United lost out to Chelsea at Old Trafford for a place in the final of the Carling Cup. Ferguson conceded that European and league aspirations took precedence. Scholes dipped into another goalscoring drought but United as a whole were firing on all cylinders, scoring four past Arsenal at Highbury, capped brilliantly by John O'Shea in the closing minutes.

Successive 2–0 victories over Manchester City and Everton followed before a heavyweight Champions League clash with AC Milan in the last 16 of the competition. City manager Kevin Keegan told the *Manchester Evening News* that Scholes could prove to be the difference between United and Chelsea in the battle for Premier League dominance.

'United are very similar to Chelsea when both sides are at full strength,' he said. 'Chelsea have John Terry, who is a rock, United have Rio Ferdinand. Chelsea have Claude Makalele who does simple things very well and United have Roy Keane. There is Duff and Robben for Chelsea, Ronaldo and Giggs for United. What United have got that Chelsea haven't is Paul Scholes.

'I think he is different to anything else in English football. He links midfield to attack and can score goals as well. He is a clever player and can find some wonderful positions. He has chosen not to play for England again and I respect his choice but out of all the good players England have, they have not got any better than him at what he does.'

United were at far from full strength against the Milan powerhouse and there was no place for van Nistelrooy in the starting line-up as United's young guns lined up against the experienced Rossoneri, who boasted a wealth of experience in Clarence Seedorf, Paulo Maldini, Rui Costa and Cafu. The home side went toe to toe with their much-lauded opponents but were undone by a lapse in concentration by goalkeeper Roy Carroll, who let in Hernan Crespo for an easy finish to give the Italians a 1–0 lead to take back to Milan.

The result meant United would have to score at the imposing San Siro to force extra time and book their place in the quarter-finals of the competition. In between the two legs United picked up four points with 2–1 victory over Portsmouth and a surprising goalless draw with Crystal Palace.

Ferguson knew he was building a new side, centred on the blossoming duo of Wayne Rooney and Cristiano Ronaldo, but their lack of experience was exploited by Milan, who sent United crashing out of the tournament with a professional, solid performance – with another goal from Argentinian Crespo, securing a 2–0 aggregate win. Scholes, Keane and Giggs would serve a crucial purpose in moulding and shaping Ferguson's new side, passing on their experience to the new crop of youngsters, and striker Ruud van Nistelrooy remained philosophical after the defeat.

'We have a younger side than Milan,' he told the *Manchester Evening News*. 'I think the experience they have was an advantage for them, and the decisive moments showed that. For us now, we learned and the younger lads got great experience and we can go on and build on this. We showed we are not far off and there is a few things to improve and that is what we want to achieve.'

Ferguson echoed his forward's sentiments, adding, 'I am happy with the quality and age of this team. They can grow up together and get better together. In that regard, I have no complaints at all. We have made a lot of changes over the last year or so but this is a good team already and they could go on to become very successful over the next five or six years.'

While Europe represented a much tougher challenge to Manchester United, domestically they were still able to pick off the weaker sides. Scholes netted a brace as United advanced to the next round of the FA Cup with a 4–0 drubbing of Southampton at St Mary's. A comfortable victory, and a place in the latter stages of the FA Cup, was the perfect tonic for Manchester United, and Scholes admits they took inspiration from Arsenal, who saw their Champions League aspirations ended only to come roaring back with victory over Bolton.

'It was a perfect start,' Scholes confessed. 'We saw Arsenal do that at Bolton and we thought that if we got out of the blocks quickly and got an early goal it could give us a good foundation for the rest of the game. It was a good response following Europe. It was disappointing in midweek but we bounced back with a good win.'

United went on a fine end-of-season run with Scholes in the side, dropping points only in a goalless draw with Blackburn at Old Trafford as the Premier League moved into its final month. Scholes believed the young Manchester United side had the wind knocked out of their sails after crashing out of the Champions League, which had a devastating affect on their league form.

'I don't know what has been wrong this season,' he told the *Manchester Evening News.* 'We have played really well in spells, but the last few weeks have not been good enough. Since losing to Milan we seem to have lost something. The main worry has been the lack of goals and the fact that we have not been creating more chances. Winning the FA Cup would be a consolation – it is still a big competition that every team wants to win. We would rather win the league and the Champions League but the FA Cup is still important.

'We have still got the major trophies in us,' he insisted. 'We have got the talent and the depth of squad to win the league and the Champions League again. We have got young players, like Wayne Rooney and Cristiano Ronaldo, and they will be better for the experience they have had this season. The future is good for this club considering the talent we have got here. We have got the players to win the big trophies again and I am like all the other senior lads in that I want to be around to help the team do it.'

José Mourinho had delivered on his promise to bring the title to Chelsea, though few expected the Portuguese to do so in his first season in British football. Scholes admitted defeat was hard to take.

'We have not been as close to the title as we would have liked,' he told the *Sunday Express.* 'We all know that we have underachieved. We have to motivate ourselves to finish second but we know really that second is not good enough for us. We want to win the title. To try to finish second, you probably don't have the same motivation you have when you are chasing the league, but second now has to be a big thing because it means you have qualified for the Champions League.'

With an FA Cup final against Arsenal to look forward to, Scholes said it would help ease some of the pain, but he took a swipe at the brand of football Chelsea used to deliver their first championship in fifty years.

'Winning the FA Cup would be some consolation for what has happened this season. Chelsea might have taken things to another level points-wise but we don't think they play the most brilliant football that has ever been seen,' he continued. 'They would probably admit that they haven't played well in a few games but have got results. Arsenal are capable of playing good football and we did that when we were winning the league.

'I think it has been a bit different to the way Chelsea have done it. We seemed to destroy teams and Arsenal were the same. Chelsea will probably end up with more points than any of us but not playing the same way.'

Chelsea had become a very real threat to United under the tutelage of the charismatic Mourinho and bankrolled by Roman Abramovich's billions, but Scholes admits it means little to the United players. 'We don't care that Chelsea have money,' he insisted. 'It's a challenge to us to try to beat them and make sure we're challenging them all the way and hopefully pipping them. We always felt we could catch Chelsea. There is still a little bit of us that thinks that now, even though they are so far ahead.

'They would have to lose people like John Terry and Frank Lampard but you never know – they have been so influential for them. They might not win another two or three games. What

Chelsea have achieved does not daunt us. I think the belief is still within us; we simply haven't played as well as we can.'

Scholes was particularly scathing of his own form, but knew the young side would mature and challenge for all honours in the next campaign. 'My own form has not been good – disappointing really,' he said. 'I should have been doing a lot better. But I feel we have got the players to challenge next season. Wayne Rooney can do everything, and he's played in different positions this season. Every time he plays he creates something or scores a goal.' Scholes was aware that, despite an FA Cup final with Arsenal to look forward to, the season would be considered a disappointment.

'My league form has not been great,' he told the *Daily Record*. 'I have scored ten goals but it took me a while to get off the mark and overall I should be doing a lot better. You always enjoy the season more if you are winning things and winning the FA Cup would be a decent prize – but at this club we do expect more than that.'

Chapter 8

SEEING CLEARLY

'The disappointment of '99 has now gone for him.'
PAUL SCHOLES

José Mourinho had delivered on his promise to make Chelsea champions of England, and United were forced to endure the formality of a Champions League qualifier with Hungarian minnows Debrecen in early August. At thirty years old, Paul Scholes would need to make important decisions regarding the rest of his career, and, to confirm his commitment, in August he agreed a new contract with Manchester United that would run until 2009. The signing of Rooney the previous summer had allowed Scholes back into his favoured central midfield slot, with the £30 million teenager proving the perfect foil for the prolific van Nistelrooy in attack.

Keane and Scholes marshalled the middle of the park, with Ronaldo and Darren Fletcher providing the width. A trip to Old

Trafford was always going to prove too much for Debrecen, and goals from Rooney, van Nistelrooy and Ronaldo put United in firm control of the two-legged tie. League affairs started five days later with a trip to Goodison Park. Van Nistelrooy edged the visitors in front on the stroke of half time before Rooney made the points safe with an emotional goal against his boyhood club. Van Nistelrooy scored the only goal of a tight encounter with Aston Villa at Old Trafford to maintain United's 100 per cent start to the campaign before another 3–0 victory over Debrecen, which confirmed their place in the group stages of the Champions League. A comfortable 2–0 win at St James' Park made it three wins and three clean sheets as United kept pace with champions Chelsea. Van Nistelrooy and Rooney bagged both goals in the second half to silence the Toon Army.

Scholes next saw league action in the first Manchester derby of the campaign at Old Trafford in September. It was van Nistelrooy again who clinically put the hosts ahead, only for Joey Barton to level the scores for City with a quarter of an hour remaining. It was a disappointing draw against their bitter rivals and allowed Chelsea to edge away at the top of the Premier League.

United were drawn against Spanish side Villarreal, Benfica of Portugal and surprise French side Lille in the group stages, which started with a hard-earned goalless draw at El Madrigal on 14 September. The Yellow Submarines boasted former Red Diego Forlán among their ranks, but the Uruguayan could not force a goal against his former employers. United's barren spell in front of goal continued against Liverpool, but a point and clean sheet at Anfield represented a good day's work for Scholes and co.

The Reds, though, were to suffer their first league defeat of the campaign at the hands of Mark Hughes's Blackburn Rovers, with Norwegian winger Morten Gamst Pedersen netting either side of a Ruud van Nistelrooy strike to silence the stunned Old Trafford crowd. Ferguson's side did not have to wait long for redemption, with the midweek Champions League encounter against Benfica giving them the opportunity to return to winning ways.

Ryan Giggs had put the hosts ahead just before half time, only to have his effort cancelled out by Liverpool target Simão. It was van Nistelrooy again who came to United's rescue, netting five minutes from time to provide a welcome three points. Goals were not hard to come by in their next league encounter at Craven Cottage on 1 October, as a thrilling contest in west London eventually saw the visitors take all three points. Scholes was a late substitute for van Nistelrooy, who bagged a brace to set United on their way to victory.

Scholes was restored to the starting line-up for the trip to Sunderland, where goals from Rooney, van Nistelrooy and Rossi gave the visitors a 3–1 win. Champions League action returned to Old Trafford with many expecting a comfortable home victory over Lille. Scholes was shown a red card for two poorly timed challenges that were the pinnacle of a bad night for Manchester United. Scholes's misery was compounded in the 63rd minute after he'd felled Jean Makoun, an act that earned him a second yellow.

Alex Ferguson, meanwhile, criticised the Lille players for their heavy-handed approach to the match. 'We have had punches in the back, kicks, elbows in the face and Ryan Giggs has got a fractured cheekbone but the player is not booked,' fumed the Scot. 'We maybe could have got a goal, but, I suppose with ten men and the other team entrenched in their own half still with one up front, they went for a point and got it.'

Old Trafford bore witness to another disappointing draw as Jermaine Jenas salvaged a point for Spurs after Mikaël Silvestre had bundled United ahead. As October drew to a close United endured a nightmare trip to The Riverside, as Scholes and his fellow players were routed 4–1 by Steve McClaren's side. Jimmy-Floyd Hasselbaink, Yakubu and a Gaizka Mendieta brace did the damage, while Ronaldo scored a late consolation for the visitors.

After the match club captain Roy Keane launched a stinging tirade on many of the Manchester United players for having no pride in the shirt. Defender Rio Ferdinand said he had to agree with the outspoken Irishman. 'He was specifically looking at faults in the Middlesbrough game regarding all the players, and he was absolutely spot on,' he said.

The result would have done much to buoy Chelsea's spirit ahead of their trip to Old Trafford on 6 November, but a looping Darren Fletcher header settled a tight encounter to inflict Chelsea's first defeat of the season and enable the Reds to make up some ground on the leaders. Ferdinand, who had committed himself to a new contract along with Scholes in the summer, admitted that the important win was a tribute to Ferguson.

'We all know what a great manager he is and beating Chelsea was for him as much as anyone,' he told the Associated Press news agency. 'It was a big, big win for the fans, the players and the manager. Everyone has been under pressure but probably no one more than the gaffer. Chelsea are a quality side but the message has gone out there to say if you play your football you have got a chance of winning against them.'

A confident victory over Charlton at The Valley followed before another disappointing goalless draw in Europe – at home to Villarreal. Scholes was one of six players booked in the match as United struggled to break down the Spaniards on their own soil in a result that left their qualification for the knockout stages hanging in the balance. Scholes helped United to victories over West Ham and Portsmouth before the trip to Benfica on 7 December.

The team warmed up for the vital European game with a confident performance in the late kick-off against Portsmouth on 3 December. Scholes made it two goals in two games as he gave United the lead on twenty minutes, but, despite dominating for large parts of the game, they were forced to wait until the eightieth minute to find a second, with Wayne Rooney bagging another. Ruud van Nistelrooy made the result safe six minutes from time as United's focus switched purely to domestic honours.

Scholes found the back of the net for the second game running to break the deadlock on six minutes. The Portuguese side rallied and drew level on 16 minutes before Beto's strike on the half-hour, which proved to be the match-winner for Benfica. The game became increasingly ill-tempered and Cristiano Ronaldo, playing in front of the arch enemies of former club Sporting Lisbon, endured a torrid afternoon, culminating in his 67th-minute substitution, much to the delight of the baying Benfica support.

United could not force an equaliser and crashed out of Europe before the turn of the year, the first time they had done so since 1995. Assistant manager Carlos Queiroz insisted supporters should wait until the end of the season before judging the team's overall performance. 'We know that everyone who loves the club is not happy because we didn't get there, but it is important to remember where we are,' he said at a press conference after the defeat. 'At the moment we are second in the Premiership and are still in the Carling and FA Cups. Those are the situations we can control and it is only at the end of the season when you will be able to judge whether Manchester United have been successful or not.

'You cannot be professional or a champion in football and only be ready to face the beautiful moments in life,' he continued. 'You have to be ready to rebound from these bad moments, accept the criticism and learn from it. But I'm convinced some of the rubbish being said about us will only make us stronger. We had a very disappointing ten- or fifteen-minute spell against Benfica, and when we look back on one more goal scored, or one fewer conceded in the Champions League it could have made all the difference. We cannot change that now. We just have to keep reminding the players and the fans we are playing well.

'For the first two or three months of this season we had an average of seven players missing through injury. When we played Benfica at home in September we were without nine important players. We are disappointed about what happened in the Champions League but we are still in a position to fight for three major trophies. Under those circumstances, why shouldn't we believe in our players? We are performing well, the team is progressing and we trust the quality of our preparation. This is not a time for talking, or finding explanations or excuses. Now it is time to move forward and deliver.'

United hosted Everton at Old Trafford four days later but were unable to find a winner after Ryan Giggs cancelled out James McFadden's sixth-minute opener. The Reds enjoyed a more confident showing at home to Wigan Athletic, with two goals in each half ensuring a comfortable 4-0 victory. Scholes was replaced by South Korean Park Ji-Sung with a quarter of an hour remaining, but the damage had already been done against Paul Jewell's Wigan.

With the demanding festive schedule approaching, United were hitting a rich vein of form at a crucial time and continued their momentum with a 2-0 victory over Aston Villa at Villa Park. Wayne Rooney netted a tenth-minute opener and van Nistelrooy made the points safe shortly after the restart. This was followed by a Boxing Day clash with relegation-haunted West Bromwich Albion at Old Trafford, and Scholes netted his third of the season with a typically classy finish after 35 minutes. Rio Ferdinand made it two with his second in a matter of weeks while, predictably, van Nistelrooy got in on the act to complete the scoring. Scholes was replaced on the hour mark by Alan Smith with a number of tricky fixtures around the New Year period still ahead, including a clash with Birmingham in the second city two days later.

On the domestic front Manchester United were flying, sweeping away the competition, and were on a run of four straight league wins over the Christmas period, going into the game with Birmingham on 28 December. United had taken the lead through Ruud van Nistelrooy on five minutes, only to be pegged back by Jamie Clapham a quarter of an hour later. Wayne Rooney restored United's advantage after the interval, only for Walter Pandiani to level the scores on 78 minutes.

After the goal, Scholes was concerned at blurred vision he had begun to suffer during the game, as he told the *Guardian*. 'I can remember it clearly,' he recalled. 'In the last ten minutes I could see a ball coming towards me, then it suddenly felt like there were three or four balls coming towards me. I thought I just had a migraine. But I went to see a specialist when it hadn't gone and they found a problem after that.

'It is worrying, not just as a footballer but also a person with a family. They thought it was quite serious at first and were asking me for my family's medical history, talking about whether there was a history of bleeding or heart disease, stuff like that. They diagnosed what the problem was and there was a small chance, I believe, it could have ended my career.'

The eye problem continued to concern specialists. 'We sent Paul to the best man in Manchester who is world-renowned,' Sir Alex Ferguson told the *Independent*. 'But we still haven't got clarification. There is no absolute medical opinion about what is going wrong so we are guessing. The specialist suggested we get a second opinion. We will send him somewhere else and see if they can diagnose something we can treat. You cannot take a chance on that even though he is not in great pain or anything.'

The mystery ailment struck a blow to Manchester United, as three goals in all competitions in December had helped maintain the Reds' challenge. And with Alan Smith and Park Ji-Sung also facing lengthy injury layoffs, Ferguson was facing a midfield crisis – with Darren Fletcher the only recognised central midfielder at his disposal. The Glazer family opened the family coffers to bring in defensive pairing Patrice Evra and Nemanja Vidić in the January transfer window, splashing out around £12 million for the pair.

Scholes was forced to spend months on the sidelines while his teammates fought valiantly to wrestle the title from José Mourinho's Chelsea. By April Scholes said his condition had started to improve. 'I still have a bit of blurred vision in my right eye but I am starting to step up training and I just want to get myself ready for next season,' he told the *Manchester Evening News*. 'Obviously you are concerned originally when you are told it is serious and you have to rest. But in my own mind I was always confident I would be back playing again. I know that is not definite yet, but I am pretty sure it will happen. I don't know whether the vision in the eye will be completely clear ever again but whatever vision I have left in the right eye I would still be able to play. It is not clear but I can see enough to play football.'

In Scholes's absence Manchester United continued to falter, losing ground on the seemingly relentless Chelsea with devastating derby defeats to Manchester City, Liverpool and

Blackburn Rovers. The title was eventually decided in late April at Stamford Bridge. Three goals without reply may have flattered the west Londoners on the day, but with an unbeaten home record Mourinho's side were worthy winners.

United found some crumb of comfort in picking up the League Cup with a crushing 4–0 victory against Wigan Athletic at Cardiff's Millennium Stadium, but a solitary piece of silverware would not satisfy the insatiable appetite for success at the club. Wayne Rooney bagged a brace while Cristiano and Louis Saha each rippled the net in a one-sided affair. Ferguson sensed an opportunity to gain something from the season and fielded a strong line-up for the clash, with Ruud van Nistelrooy the only notable absentee in a formidable-looking side. Only the week before, United's FA Cup campaign had ended at the hands of Liverpool at Anfield at the fifth-round stage.

With the title already out of their grasp, Manchester United looked to end the season on a high in front of their own fans with the visit of Charlton Athletic on the final day of the season. Scholes made his long-overdue return to first-team action as a substitute for John O'Shea. The hosts had built up a healthy half-time lead with goals from Louis Saha and Cristiano Ronaldo and a Jason Euell own goal. Kieran Richardson bagged a rare goal in a United shirt on the hour mark as Ferguson's side signed off their season with a stylish performance.

Chelsea, meanwhile, were celebrating consecutive league titles, boosted by Roman Abramovich's millions and 'The Chosen One'. According to Scholes, two years without lifting the Premier League would not suffice for a club of Manchester

United's stature and he called for a vast improvement in the next campaign.

'The last couple of seasons we let Chelsea get too far ahead of us and we could never peg them back,' he told the *Guardian*. 'That wasn't fun. It might be good enough for some clubs to finish second or third but it isn't for us, and you don't enjoy those moments.'

Alex Ferguson was confident of having the marauding midfielder at his disposal for the 2006–07 season as he plotted the downfall of Abramovich's Chelsea Empire. 'We are convinced he will be back next season,' Ferguson told the official Manchester United magazine. 'He is a sensational player, one of the best we have ever had. It must have been worrying for Paul because, when you have a problem with blurred vision and nobody can really give you a reason for it, then it is a concern. But fortunately he got back into training; he played the second half of the last game of the season against Charlton and did well.'

Manchester United finished the season in second place, eight points off leaders Chelsea and just a point above bitter rivals Liverpool, while Arsène Wenger's Arsenal were made to settle for fourth. Ferguson's side lost only once at Old Trafford, with Blackburn Rovers doing a league double over the Reds that season and, despite the considerable presence of Ruud van Nistelrooy and Wayne Rooney, a lack of cutting edge meant five home draws were seen as points lost.

The summer of 2006 saw Germany host the World Cup, the first international tournament Scholes had not been involved in since Euro '96. Sven-Göran Eriksson had an impressive first elevem on paper, but the midfield pairing of Frank Lampard and Steve Gerrard had yet to gel, and Scholes said he was pleased to get a rest when internationals came around. 'I think the break has been beneficial,' he told the *Guardian*. 'It did refresh me and I had a lot of time to think about everything. I know I can't go on much longer, maybe another two or three years, so I just have to enjoy it now.'

Manchester United invested heavily in the summer, splashing out around £18 million to lure Michael Carrick from White Hart Lane with the hope of finding a successor to Roy Keane, a void they had been unable to fill the previous season. Carrick was a graduate of the West Ham youth system that brought through Joe Cole, Frank Lampard and Rio Ferdinand – all established England internationals – and Scholes said United had made another quality signing in the Geordie.

'He has been a great signing for us and I think he has really helped,' he told Manchester United's website. 'His passing is brilliant, most people see that straight away, and not just that, he works hard for the team as well. It's been nice because he is so composed and calm on the ball. It has been really enjoyable and I think we have developed a good understanding. Hopefully that will continue.'

Carrick, though blessed with a terrific eye for a pass, was not the midfield bulldozer of Roy Keane, but Scholes believed he could grow into that role. 'I don't know if he is that much of a different player to Roy,' he continued. 'They play a similar role. It is difficult to compare him to other players – I don't look at it like that. I know that I can play alongside him and I feel comfortable alongside him in the team. He has got all the capabilities of a top midfielder and that is what you need at this club.'

The new signing would add a new dimension to the Manchester United midfield but Scholes felt his role would not change to accommodate the former Spur.

'Our job is the same as it has been when I have played with anyone else in midfield: get the ball to our most dangerous players in attacking positions. If we can do that then we have got every chance of winning games because of the quality of our attacking players. I suppose he has freed me up a little bit to try to get forward more. I know he doesn't get forward that often. But he can do that, he is definitely capable of scoring goals. He is more of a sitting midfielder, so he takes on that role and I can get forward.'

Ferguson was charged with ending Chelsea's two-year reign as Premier League champions and the west London side had certainly spent big in the summer, acquiring Ukrainian hit man Andriy Shevchenko for £30 million, while German captain Michael Ballack's wages alone would empty most clubs' coffers. Ferguson, meanwhile, was much happier to have Scholes back in his side after missing the majority of the last season, something, he said, that would make him more at ease with the upcoming Premier League campaign.

'I am more confident now that Scholes is coming back,' he told *The Times*. 'He brings a bit of class at important times in games. That's what Scholes is probably best at: producing moments that can turn games – so it is a big bonus to have him back. One of his biggest assets has been appearing in the box late.'

Ferguson knew that his maturing side needed only minor changes to mould them into champions, and, not wanting to upset the gentle learning curve for his young team, made just the one splash in the summer transfer window with the acquisition of Carrick. There was, however, one major departure from the Old Trafford ranks as Ruud van Nistelrooy, Manchester United's most prolific striker, made the switch to Real Madrid for a small fee that did not represent his goals-to-games ratio in a United shirt. A rift had developed between van Nistelrooy and Ferguson and, as with Jaap Stam before him, the player was offloaded in his prime.

The main talking point of the summer was United's Portuguese *wunderkind* Cristiano Ronaldo and his part in England's acrimonious departure from the World Cup in Germany. The United number seven was involved in a fracas with club mate Wayne Rooney, which cast a doubt over his future at Old Trafford after he had become England's public enemy number one. The blame for England's quarter-final defeat was laid purely at his feet, meaning Ferguson had to prove his man-management qualities once again to persuade his star asset not to jump ship. It was not the first time one of Ferguson's squad had felt the wrath of a nation: Eric Cantona was ostracised for his kung-fu kick on a Crystal Palace fan a decade before, while David Beckham had to endure months of torture following his red card against Argentina in 1998. Ronaldo opted to stay at Manchester United and weather the storm.

The season opened with the visit of Fulham to Old Trafford with the 76,000-strong crowd baying for blood after a disappointing campaign last time out. All eyes were on Rooney and Ronaldo, with many questioning whether they could work together following their summer fallout. The United fans were not to be disappointed, as United romped to a 5–1 victory over the hapless Cottagers with Ronaldo, Saha, an own goal and a Wayne Rooney brace firing United to a convincing win.

Any doubts over the cohesion in the United side were soon put to bed, with Rooney's beautifully flighted cross met on the volley by Ronaldo in a goal of such devastating efficiency that all doubts about their future were quickly shelved. There was no place for Carrick in the starting line-up as Scholes partnered John O'Shea in the centre of midfield.

Scholes played no further part in the next three matches, with a needless red card in the pre-season Amsterdam tournament earning him a three-match suspension, which stood in the Premier League. Darren Fletcher and then Michael Carrick slotted in for victories over Charlton, Watford and Tottenham Hotspur. Scholes, one of the original Fergie Fledglings, had to take a back seat as the Scot's new crop blew away the competition with three consecutive wins.

Perhaps the most popular of goals came in the victory over Charlton, where Ole Gunnar Solskjaer netted his first goal in nearly two years after a protracted injury nightmare, much to the delight of the travelling fans. Many had expected the match against newly promoted Watford to be a stroll for United. Despite a less than convincing performance, the result was the same as

United racked up another three points in a narrow 2–1 victory, with Ryan Giggs holding his nerve to slot home the winner.

After the Watford game Manchester United had amassed ten goals in their first three games, which was a stunning total when it had taken them until October to reach eight goals in the previous campaign. A blistering start was rewarded with Ryan Giggs and Alex Ferguson picking up Player and Manager of the Month awards respectively, as United surged to the top of the pile at the end of August.

'We have been maturing in the last couple of years, but now you can see the maturity more and more,' Ferguson told the Associated Press. 'The likes of Ronaldo, Fletcher and Park Ji-Sung are all growing up. Ronaldo has really matured.'

Ferguson had thrown down the gauntlet to champions Chelsea with their best start to a league campaign in 21 years. Manchester United were drawn alongside Celtic, FC Copenhagen and old enemies Benfica in their Champions League group as they looked to avenge their embarrassing early defeat at the hands of the Portuguese side in the last campaign.

Scholes returned in time for United's Champions League opener against Celtic at Old Trafford on 13 September. The hosts had fallen behind to a goal from Jan Vennegoor of Hesselink, but a Louis Saha double swung the match in United's favour. It was Scholes's vision that set up the French striker to net the equaliser, as his superbly weighted through ball gave Saha an easy chance to move the hosts on level terms. However, Shunsuke Nakamura curled the Scottish champions on to level pegging before Ole Solskjaer's second of the season wrapped up the points for Ferguson's side.

Despite their flying start to domestic affairs the visit of Arsenal proved too much for United, with Emanuel Adebayor pouncing in the first half with the only goal of a tight encounter at Old Trafford. United found themselves under the cosh for large periods of the match and Scholes had to be alert to clear a goal-bound header off the line after a fumble from goalkeeper Tomasz Kuszczak, who made his Manchester United debut. The Polish stopper saved a penalty, but was helpless as the lanky Togo striker prodded the ball home from close range.

Defeat to their rivals was hard to take after such a dominant start and their bad luck continued at the Madejski Stadium as Premier League newcomers Reading fought and scrapped for a well-earned point in front of their delirious support, who could scarcely believe they had held the champions of England on their own turf. Kevin Doyle's first-half penalty had fired the Royals ahead after Gary Neville's handball. But Cristiano Ronaldo was on hand to rescue a point with a magnificent run and shot that was past Marcus Hahnemann before he could move.

The fluency of Manchester United's attacking triumvirate of Rooney, Ronaldo and Saha began to cause all sorts of problems for opposition defences – with Wayne Rooney given licence to roam on either flank or through the middle. Scholes was an ample deputy in the wide positions when the marauding Englishman ventured through the middle. Ferguson opted for this system for the trip to Benfica as John O'Shea and Michael Carrick held the middle of the park. Manchester United were suffering another tepid away performance in Europe and were struggling against their Portuguese hosts, but, when Scholes started an incisive breakaway, Louis Saha took control and fired in a deflected winner to give Ferguson his first away win in Europe for three years.

Domestic bliss continued with a 2–0 victory over Newcastle at St James' Park, with Solskjaer again proving his predatory skills as he reacted first after Ronaldo's drive hit the post. The Norwegian striker bagged a second after Nemanja Vidić tame effort hit his side, wrong-footing a hapless Steve Harper before nestling in the bottom corner.

On 14 October United travelled to the JJB Stadium to face Paul Jewell's Wigan Athletic. Left-back Leighton Baines fired in a wicked free kick to give Wigan a shock first-half lead and Manchester United worked hard to get an equaliser. They were forced to wait until deep into the second half before a Vidić header levelled the scores. Luis Saha gave the visitors the lead and Solskjaer made the points safe with another timely intervention.

Champions League action continued with the visit of Copenhagen to Old Trafford, and Scholes got his first goal of the season with a now trademark strike to break the deadlock. The former England winger hit a sweet strike past the goalkeeper's despairing dive from outside the box to set Manchester United on their way to a comfortable evening against the Danish minnows. John O'Shea doubled the advantage with a fortunate deflection before a late Kieran Richardson effort made it three.

Scholes had now been a Manchester United mainstay for the best part of a decade and brought up his 500th appearance in the famous red jersey fittingly, against bitter rivals Liverpool at Old Trafford. With the spotlight on the Salford-born midfielder, no one thought to tell the Liverpool defender, who allowed him to ghost in unmarked to break the deadlock with a bundled finish to give United the lead in the first half. An incredible strike from Rio Ferdinand made the points safe as the hosts gained a massive boost with victory over their old enemy.

Scholes received the man-of-the-match award for his display but was, inevitably, gone before the media could have a chance to interview him. 'He's not really bothered about personal accolades, to be honest with you,' Rio Ferdinand told Sky Sports after the game. 'But, rightly so, he's man of the match. He has shown how much we missed him last season.'

At the age of 31 Scholes had proved himself a symbol of Sir Alex Ferguson's past glories, and proved he could still represent future success for the Scot as he searched for that elusive second Champions League win. 'I had a feeling Scholes would score and it was probably written in the script,' the Scot told the Associated Press. 'But he really deserves it and it was a great moment for him to score such an important goal against his deadliest rivals.'

Ferguson lauded Scholes for his impact since returning from his lengthy injury layoff. 'There was a concern when he got his eye injury and we were so relieved when it just seemed to disappear as quickly as it came,' he told MUTV.

In typically modest fashion, Scholes played down his milestone achievement, insisting that personal accolades did not interest him too much. 'It was good to get there,' he told MUTV. 'And to score a goal on the day as well made it extra special, but it's just another game whether it is your five hundredth, one hundredth or fiftieth. I don't think it makes much difference – it's just a number.'

Scholes had joined a select group of Manchester United players to breach the 500-games mark alongside legends Bobby Charlton, Billy Foulkes and current teammate Ryan Giggs. However, with the Premier League campaign well under way, there was to be no time to rest on personal achievements, as a trip to the Reebok Stadium would be a test of strength for Ferguson's young side.

Wayne Rooney netted his first goal since the opening day of the season to set United on their way to a comfortable 4–0 win in the week the young prodigy turned 21. A terrific result in the local derby was followed up by a shock defeat in Copenhagen as the Reds suffered their first defeat in the Champions League group stages. The Danes netted a solitary goal to which United could find no answer.

Their next league match against Portsmouth at Old Trafford marked Ferguson's twentieth anniversary at the helm of Manchester United – a trophy-laden spell that had made it the biggest club in the world. The players responded to the great occasion with a 3–0 drubbing of the Hampshire club before surrendering their League Cup crown at Southend, courtesy of a Freddy Eastwood goal. However, in the league Manchester United were an altogether different proposition and their stunning run continued with victory over Blackburn Rovers, who had become a bogey side since former Red Mark Hughes took control at Ewood Park. Louis Saha once again demonstrated his early form with the only goal to settle the Lancashire derby.

United travelled to newly promoted Sheffield United on 18 November, having not conceded a goal since the game at the JJB in mid-October, but were forced to fight and scrap for three points against Neil Warnock's side. Scholes's former youth team friend Keith Gillespie broke the deadlock for the Blades, the first they had conceded in five matches, before a Wayne Rooney brace swung the match in United's favour. Another disappointing European away day ended in defeat at Celtic Park, with Japanese hotshot Shunsuke Nakamura striking another beautiful free kick after a soft foul on Czech midfielder Jiří Jarošík, which left the final group game against Benfica as do or die for Manchester United, who faced the prospect of early defeat at the hands of the Portuguese side once again.

But first there was the small matter of the summit meeting between Manchester United and Chelsea at Old Trafford, which pitted the reigning champions against the league leaders. Saha's calm, side-footed finish gave United the lead after Scholes's measured through ball, only for Ricardo Carvalho to rescue a point with a header.

A rare goal from left-back Patrice Evra, his first for the club, capped a fine performance as Manchester United moved three points clear at the top of the table with a 3–0 victory over Everton.

Next up was a trip to the Riverside, where Middlesbrough had proved formidable opposition in recent years. Louis Saha scored from the spot to atone for his Celtic Park nightmare, where his penalty miss had cost United a point a month before. Darren Fletcher netted a rare goal to restore United's lead, with victory putting Ferguson's side ten points better off then they were this time the previous year.

The crucial game against Benfica followed in midweek with Manchester United knowing they had to avoid defeat to make it through to the knockout stages. The match got off to a disastrous start for Manchester United when Nelson's sweetly struck goal gave the visitors the lead. The game proved to be a test of United's mettle and they passed with flying colours with Vidić, Ryan Giggs and Louis Saha putting them through to the last 16 of the Champions League, much to the relief of the increasingly nervy Old Trafford faithful.

Revenge would prove sweet for Manchester United both in Europe and at home as derby ghosts were finally exorcised with a convincing 3–1 victory over Manchester City. Rooney, Saha and Ronaldo all found the back of the net as United moved a massive nine points clear at the top of the table at the start of December.

The momentum was with Ferguson's side going into the Christmas period, but a surprise defeat to West Ham took the wind out of their sails. The match at the Boleyn Ground was Alan Curbishley's first in charge of the Hammers under Eggert Magnússon's regime, and the former Charlton boss got the right reaction from his side, who edged the game 1–0 thanks to Nigel Reo-Coker's scrappy winner.

The result proved only a temporary setback as a storming 3–0 victory over Aston Villa in the second city ensured United stayed top at Christmas. Ronaldo fired the visitors ahead with Manchester United's 2,000th goal under Sir Alex Ferguson. The 2001st, however, would prove to be one of the finest the Scot had seen in his two decades at Old Trafford as Scholes fired in his contender for goal of the season. Ryan Giggs's corner had been headed clear by the Villa defence and the ball dropped to Scholes well outside the box. Without a moment's hesitation he volleyed the ball past Gábor Kiraly with such devastating force and accuracy that it was past the Hungarian goalkeeper before he dived. It was a sensational strike and certainly one of Scholes's best in a Manchester United shirt.

Defender Rio Ferdinand told MUTV he feared the strike might even outshine his goal against Liverpool earlier in the season. 'This year he's come back like nothing was wrong with him,' said the former Leeds defender. 'He's rivalling me for goal of the season, although I think I've just pipped him! But he is a joy to play with and a joy to watch.'

Scholes, meanwhile, told Manchester United's website that he loves taking up that position on the edge of the box, where he can pick up the loose ball and try his luck from range – but it is not a move they try out in training. 'It's not something we have worked on too much,' he said. 'You just know that corners are very often cleared to the edge of the box. It's a position I enjoy taking up because you are always hoping the ball will come out to you so you get a shot on goal. Wayne is the same as well. He loves shooting, so he is normally there queuing up to have a go. Both of us are hoping the ball comes to one of us, if we have not already scored from a header because Rio and Vidić are so dangerous at set pieces.'

Manchester United's Boxing Day fixture gave them another tricky tie against Wigan, and the league leaders were reliant on substitute Cristiano Ronaldo to come off the bench and end the stubborn resistance from Paul Jewell's side. The Portuguese winger made a difference having been on the pitch only a minute as he slotted home a penalty after Park was felled in the area. Ronaldo bagged a brace before Ole Solskjaer made the points safe.

While often in blistering form for large parts of the season, United seemed to struggle against teams they would usually be expected to roll over, and the same was true with Reading's visit to Old Trafford on 30 December. Solskjaer scored again to break the deadlock before Ibrahima Sonko levelled with a header before a Ronaldo brace gave the hosts breathing space. Lira Lita netted a scrappy late goal to ensure an uncomfortable last few minutes, but United held out to remain six points clear at the top of the league at the end of 2006.

With clear daylight between Sir Alex Ferguson's Reds and second-placed Chelsea going into 2007, Paul Scholes stressed the importance of winning the Premier League and ending Chelsea's two-year reign as champions of England. 'It has to be our top priority,' he told Manchester United's official website. 'After not doing so well in the Premiership in the last couple of years we are all more determined than ever to lift the trophy this year.

'The league is the major trophy, your bread and butter. We have not had the trophy for four years now, that's too long and it is a trophy we desperately want to win back. The other competitions would be a bonus if we can do well in them. If we could win all three that would be nice, but, if I had to choose one, it would be the league, and I think a lot of the players feel that way. To do it, whenever you do it, is a massive accomplishment. It has become more difficult to win; you would have to say that.

'Arsenal and Chelsea in the last three seasons have performed so well that you need to be more consistent. But winning the league is a fantastic achievement any time you do it because it is recognition for your performances over the course of the entire season.'

Scholes felt that being top of the league and playing such devastating attacking football showed that Manchester United had the potential to do great things under Ferguson. 'The league tells you everything you need to know. If you look at the points total and the goal difference column, it's a good attacking team that can defend as well. We've kept clean sheets and scored a lot of goals. I think there's a really good balance to this team. That's what you need to be successful. So in that sense it's similar to the other successful United sides I've played in. It's a different team, but what's stayed the same is the type of football we play – always looking to score goals and keeping it tight at the back.

'In the most successful teams we've always looked to score goals and, if you look at some of the players we have going forward, players like Cristiano, Wayne, Louis, Ryan, that is certainly the case with the team now. Even the defenders are scoring as well!'

The remarkable comeback by Ole Gunnar Solskjaer, ending his injury hell, had given United another option in attack, and had boosted the size of their squad, which is a necessity when fighting for three different trophies. Ferguson was given the luxury of being able to rotate his squad, with players such as Darren Fletcher and John O'Shea proving worthy deputies when called upon to fill in for the first-team regulars.

Two thousand and seven began with a trip to St James' Park to take on Newcastle as United attempted to get the New Year off to a blistering start. They were to be found wanting, however, when James Milner fired in a stunning goal to give Newcastle the lead. However, Scholes was on hand to equalise, showing quick feet in the edge of the area before prodding past Shay Given with a measured finish from 18 yards. He was not finished there either, as he struck a firm effort that went straight through Given to haul the visitors ahead, only for debutant David Edgar to slide home a late equaliser to leave the game deadlocked at two each.

Ferguson had assessed his options and made a rare foray into the transfer market during the January window and brought in Swedish striker Henrik Larsson, a former Celtic legend north of the border. Ferguson believed the next three months would prove critical in deciding the outcome of the season and swooped to take Larsson from Swedish club Helsingborg until March. The move brought instant rewards as Larsson marked his debut with a goal against Aston Villa as United's FA Cup campaign began at Old Trafford. The Swede pounced after neat interplay before stabbing past Gabor Kiraly from inside the box. Substitute Milan Baroš looked to have sent the tie to a replay when he slid the ball past Edwin van der Sar, but Ole Solskjaer had other ideas, with his late effort escaping Kiraly's clutches to send United through to the next round.

After the agony of late defeat in the Cup, Villa were forced to return to Old Trafford for a league fixture, and were found wanting again as United strolled to a 3–1 victory. A typical raking pass from Scholes set United on their way, as Park eventually capitalised on a slick counterattack from the hosts. The Korean then fed Michael Carrick to double the advantage only a minute later. A Cristiano Ronaldo header made the points safe as United claimed their first league win of 2007.

However, they were to be the victims of late heartbreak in the next league fixture, with a first trip to Arsenal's new Emirates Stadium. A Wayne Rooney header gave United the lead only for Robin van Persie to fire home an equaliser after Scholes had been bundled over in the Manchester United half. A draw at the Gunners would have been a good result, but Thierry Henry's last minute header stole all three points for Arsène Wenger's side.

A first defeat of 2007 had to be put out of mind for the visit of Portsmouth in the FA Cup. United had two goals harshly ruled out by the officials before Rooney finally broke the deadlock. The England striker capped a marvellous performance with a devastating, magical chip over David James to double the lead. Pedro Mendes fired in a late consolation strike but United clung on to advance to the next round.

Watford were next up to try their luck at Old Trafford, which was quickly becoming a fortress for the home side, and so it proved again, as Aidy Boothroyd's side were blown away by the insatiable Wayne Rooney. A Cristiano Ronaldo penalty and an own-goal had fired United into a comfortable 2–0 lead before

Rooney got in on the act with a composed side-foot finish over the onrushing goalkeeper to cap a fine performance.

Scholes was on the scoresheet again as United tore into Tottenham Hotspur at White Hart Lane. Another Ronaldo penalty and a Vidić header had put United ahead, before Scholes popped up with a pinpoint run to force the ball over the line after terrific build-up play from Ronaldo. Ryan Giggs made it 4–0 as the Reds continued their rehabilitation following the devastating defeat to Arsenal in north London. The momentum continued with the visit of Charlton Athletic to Old Trafford and, when Park climbed highest to head home, there was going to be only one winner. Fletcher made it two after being teed up by Wayne Rooney, who was entering a rich vein of form.

FA Cup adventures continued with another home tie, this time against Reading, who had posed United problems in the league and the same was true in the Cup. Carrick's low, drilled effort broke the deadlock before Iceland international Brynjar Gunnarsson rescued a point. Goalkeeping deputy Adam Federici would win Player of the Round for his heroics in the Reading goal, frustrating the home crowd with a string of fine saves to take the tie to a Madejski Stadium replay.

Cup games were coming thick and fast for Scholes with the first knockout round of the Champions League pitting United against Lille, who had proved awkward opposition in the past. An ill-tempered game was capped when Ryan Giggs took a quick free kick, which bamboozled the home defence, who had not had time to form ranks before the Welshman clipped the ball into the bottom corner. Lille's players threatened to walk off the pitch in a petulant act in protest at the goal, but the goal stood, and United had a one-goal lead to take back to Old Trafford.

The following league game, against Fulham, proved a massive test of their mettle, as it looked destined for a draw after Giggs had volleyed United onto level terms. However, another moment of divine intervention from Cristiano Ronaldo won the game in the 88th minute, with the Portuguese ramming home a deflected shot to give Ferguson's side all three points, much to the relief of the Manchester United bench. The win over Fulham had opened up a nine-point lead for United at the top of the Premier League, but there was still a job to be done against Reading in the FA Cup, which produced a fantastic spectacle for the neutral but would have done little for the nerves of the travelling United fans.

With United still going strong on three fronts, a trip to Anfield would prove a big test for their title credentials. After the euphoria of the previous encounter between the two sides for Scholes, the return fixture would prove less fruitful. Scholes chased a loose ball with Spanish playmaker Xabi Alonso and led with an elbow, which caught the former Real Sociedad star. The referee, backed by 40,000 screaming Scousers, showed a straight red card as Scholes faced the horror of a sending-off against his bitter personal rivals. The Northwest derby continued in a typically cagey manner and saw the visitors soak up the Liverpool pressure for large parts of the match. However, John O'Shea proved the unlikely match winner as he kept a cool head to slot home in the dying moments. Ferguson's side were looking like potential champions, winning scruffy matches with late goals, buoyed by their never-say-die attitude, but for Scholes another lapse in concentration had earned him another spell in the stands as the race for the title gathered pace.

Domestic suspension did not stop Scholes from taking part in the home leg of their Champions League knockout tie with Lille, who were still smarting from their acrimonious defeat across the Channel. Henrik Larsson was making his farewell appearance in front of the home fans, as his three-month loan spell would soon be coming to an end. Acquiring the Swede had proved a magnificent bit of business by Alex Ferguson, as Larsson netted crucial goals while enabling the club's strikers to have a rest. It was fitting, then, that Larsson netted the only goal of the game to send United through to the quarter-finals with a comfortable, if uninspiring, 2–0 aggregate win.

The draw for the last eight of the Champions League pitted Ferguson's men against Italian giants Roma, who were enjoying a renaissance under coach Luciano Spalletti.

Scholes took no part in the 2–2 draw with Middlesbrough in the FA Cup, with the Teessiders once again proving tough opposition for United. Goals from Lee Cattermole and George Boateng had cancelled out Rooney's opener, but the Dutchman's handball gave Cristiano Ronaldo the chance to score from the spot. The Portuguese made no mistake, and sent the tie to an Old Trafford replay. The match, however, saw United sustain further injury woes as Gary Neville was forced off with an ankle injury that would see the captain spend a long time in the treatment room.

United continued their title charge after cruising past Bolton 3–1 at Old Trafford. Park put the hosts ahead before a counterattack of devastating fluency between Ronaldo and

Rooney saw the Englishman double the lead. The insatiable Rooney then grabbed a second before Gary Speed's consolation penalty. Scholes sat out the last game of his suspension as United finally saw off Middlesbrough, thanks to a solitary Cristiano Ronaldo goal.

Scholes returned to the Manchester United side on the last day of March and his return reaped instant rewards, as Mark Hughes's Blackburn Rovers were on the wrong end of an Old Trafford rout. While United looked in fine form in attack, defensive injuries continued to cause concern, with Serbian enforcer Nemanja Vidić the next player to be forced out, with a broken collarbone.

United's attacking options proved far too much for the Lancashire side as Scholes cancelled out Matt Derbyshire's opener with a sublime finish. Having picked the ball up inside the area, he showed great composure to round two defenders before slotting past Brad Friedel. Goals from Carrick, Park and Solskjaer gave United a 4–1 victory and a six-point lead at the top of the table going into the penultimate month of the football calendar.

United travelled to Rome on 4 April knowing an away goal would stand them in good stead for the return leg at Old Trafford. Fan violence marred much of the game, with heavy-handed policing causing trouble for the travelling United fanatics. There was a hostile atmosphere in the Stadio Olimpico and Scholes received his second red card in a matter of weeks, having received two harsh yellows in the opening 34 minutes. Scholes told MUTV after the game that he was given no help from the soft Italian opposition.

'I made that first tackle and I didn't really need to,' he said. 'I should have known better. We were playing away and, particularly in Italy, they like to get players booked – and I fell for it.'

United were forced to play out the remaining hour with ten men and Roma looked to take full advantage, with Rodrigo Taddei's deflected shot edging them ahead on the stroke of half time. United battled hard to stem the tide and hit Roma on the break, with a darting run from Ronaldo setting up Wayne Rooney, who slotted home after an immaculate first touch to grab the all-important away goal on the hour mark. Parity lasted only seven minutes, however, as Mirko Vučinić stole all three points, firing in after Edwin van der Sar could only parry the initial effort.

The tired Manchester United squad faced a trip to Fratton Park three days later, with Portsmouth taking full advantage of their midweek exertions, with a rare defensive lapse from Rio Ferdinand condemning the visitors to a 2–0 deficit. John O'Shea bundled in another late goal but it proved in vain, as a 2–1 defeat on the south coast blew the title race wide open once again. Suspension in the Stadio Olimpico tussle meant Scholes was forced to sit out another Champions League encounter at Old Trafford, which proved to be one of the most remarkable nights in the history of the club. Roma were defending a one-goal lead but the hosts knew they could go through with a 1–0 win, thanks to Wayne Rooney's away goal. Marshalled by the excellent Darren Fletcher and Alan Smith, United romped to an unprecedented 7–1 victory over the Italians, scything them apart with devastating attacking flair to which their defensive-minded opponents could find no answer. United had booked their place in the semi-finals of the Champions League where they would meet AC Milan, Carlo Ancelotti's European powerhouses, who would represent an altogether different challenge to their Serie A rivals.

After the euphoria of midweek the goals kept flowing for Ferguson's side, as United booked their place in the first FA Cup final to be held at the new Wembley with a 4–1 victory over Watford. Scholes was restored to the starting line up alongside Carrick in the middle of the park. The match at Villa Park proved to be a one-sided affair, as goals from Ronaldo, Richardson and a Wayne Rooney brace sent United on their way to a 4–1 win over their London opponents, who had done well to make it this far considering the exertions of their Premier League campaign.

The march towards regaining the Premier League continued with a 2–0 victory over Sheffield United at Old Trafford, with Carrick and Rooney finding the back of the net each side of half time. There was a slight stumble on 21 April, as Middlesbrough held United to a 1–1 draw at Old Trafford. Kieran Richardson had fired the home side ahead after just three minutes, but Australian striker Mark Viduka levelled the scores on forty-five minutes as Ferguson's charges remained at the summit with four games left to play.

Manchester United were given home advantage for the first leg of their clash of the titans with AC Milan on 2 May. Injury worries at the back had marred preparation for the match, with Ferguson only two games away from making his second Champions League final. Scholes was brought back into the side despite sitting out the 7–1 mauling of Roma, as Ferguson knew he needed to match Milan's wealth of experience. The home side were missing six first team regulars for the tie, while AC Milan could boast a full complement of players, including the sublime Brazilian Kaká, widely regarded as the finest player in the world. United got off to the dream start, however, as Argentinian defender Gabriel Heinze forced the ball over the line on six minutes after Dida had failed to gather Cristiano Ronaldo's header.

The Stretford End could sense another glorious European night but were forced to watch in awe at the genius of Kaká, who destroyed the United defence on his own. After collecting a routine pass on the edge of the area the Brazilian showed a devastating turn of pace to leave the centre-backs for dead before sliding past Van der Sar in a move of breathtaking beauty. He was not finished there and tormented the home side further, capitalising on defensive hesitancy to burst into the area before firing a pinpoint low drive past the reach of Van der Sar to turn the tie on its head.

United had plenty of flair in their own side and Wayne Rooney showed why he is one of the hottest properties in world football by bagging two second-half goals, including what was literally a last-minute winner, to give United a 3–2 lead after a sizzling ninety minutes of football. Old Trafford had witnessed a showcase for European football with two attacking sides jostling for a place in the grandest club match in the world – with Ferguson's side needing only a goalless draw in the San Siro a week later to book their place in the final of the Champions League.

The Professional Footballers Association voted for their team of the season, which was released at their annual dinner. Scholes was among eight Manchester United players who made up the best eleven players the Premier League could offer. Goalkeeper Edwin van der Sar and defenders Gary Neville, Nemanja Vidić, Rio Ferdinand and Patrice Evra completed a clean sweep at the back. Scholes, Giggs and Cristiano Ronaldo comprised three of the midfield as United's scintillating form won the praise of their peers.

However, Ferguson's side had won nothing yet and a difficult trip to David Moyes's rapidly improving Everton awaited. Knowing rivals Chelsea were ready to pounce on any mistake, United found themselves 2–0 down with less than 25 minutes remaining after Alan Stubbs and Manuel Fernandes had fired Everton ahead. Ferguson had left Ronaldo on the bench with half an eye on Champions League affairs, but was forced to play his trump card with Everton firmly in control.

Ronaldo proved his importance to the side as he galvanised United into action. John O'Shea halved the deficit with another poacher's goal that was becoming his trademark for the season, and a Phil Neville own goal restored parity. Defeat would have seen Chelsea move level on points if they overcame Bolton, and goals from Rooney and substitute Chris Eagles marked a stunning fightback from Manchester United.

The courage shown by the players was made all the sweeter by news of Chelsea's draw with Bolton, which gave them one hand on the Premier League title. United were now five points clear with three games to go and their relentless charge towards glory showed little sign of slowing going into May. However, domestic affairs were put to one side as United attempted to finish off the second part of their Italian job.

Milan had the bonus of two away goals and knew a 1–0 victory would see them through to the final in Athens. Ancelotti's side were insatiable, and showed their experience on the big stage with a powerful performance that blew away United's young side. Kaká returned to haunt the United defence with a clinical opener before Dutchman Clarence Seedorf fired in on the half-hour mark to double the lead.

United had offered little in attack and their misery was compounded on 78 minutes when Alberto Gilardino slotted home to make it three goals without reply. Ferguson could not hide his disappointment after the game, but conceded that his side's gruelling schedule had hampered their preparation. 'We should have seen out the first 20 minutes without cutting our throats,' he told the *Daily Mail*. 'We lost two goals very easily and at this level you have to do better in defending those situations. Milan were better prepared physically. They have been able to rest players and we have not, but I would still have expected more from my team.'

There was chance for instant retribution for Scholes as United travelled to Eastlands looking for the three points that could seal the league title. City were well aware of the damage Cristiano Ronaldo had caused in a scintillating season and employed underhanded tactics to stop him, with Michael Ball stamping on the Portuguese winger's chest, much to the chagrin of the United bench. It was fitting that Ball would give away the penalty from which Ronaldo gave United the lead, and, when Van der Sar dramatically saved a late Darius Vassell penalty, United had a nail-biting victory over their local rivals.

Chelsea's dwindling title challenge hung in the balance and needed victory in their match against Arsenal at the Emirates to stay in the hunt. However, a 1–1 draw in north London confirmed Manchester United as champions of England, ending a four-year wait for the title. José Mourinho had failed to win the Premier League for the first time in two seasons and the Blues' misery was compounded as they gave the newly crowned champions a guard of honour in the next league game at Stamford Bridge. An understrength Manchester United travelled to Stamford Bridge knowing they could not be toppled at the summit, while United fans up and down the country enjoyed John Terry and co. clapping Ferguson's side onto the pitch ahead of their drab goalless draw.

The party began at Old Trafford on the final day of the season with the visit of West Ham, who needed to win to stay in the Premier League as the fight for survival reached a dramatic climax. Carlos Tévez, a controversial loanee, scored the only goal of the game to maintain his side's Premier League status for another year. Fuelled by Eggert Magnússon's millions, the Hammers had struggled to find continuity and the signing of Tévez and countryman Javier Mascherano would cost the Hammers over £5 million for breaching Premier League rules. However, the fine was a small price to pay for avoiding the drop to the wilderness of the Championship.

The Premier League's top two would contest the first FA Cup

final to be held at the new £750 million Wembley Stadium in the mid-May sunshine. After a bruising league campaign, the two teams would face off one last time for the oldest prize in football. Under Mourinho, Chelsea were rock solid, and more than capable of soaking up pressure before hitting on the counterattack, and the Portuguese tactician used these tactics to great effect in the Wembley showpiece. With Ronaldo, Giggs and Rooney, Manchester United had more flair than any other side in Europe and Chelsea's defensive United of Claude Makalele, John Obi Mikel and John Terry had to be at their best to stifle the threat of United's attacking trio. The match inevitably went to extra time with neither side able to force a breakthrough. But, when Didier Drogba exchanged passes with Frank Lampard, he strode into the area before lifting the ball over Van der Sar to win the Cup for the Blues.

It was a sickening blow to the Reds, who had fought hard for 120 minutes to carve out an opening, only to be hit by a moment of brilliance from the Chelsea attack.

Disappointment at falling short in Cup competitions was to be short-lived, however, with the Premier League safely home in the Old Trafford trophy cabinet. Sitting deep once again, Scholes set the tempo in the middle of the park, spraying the ball at will to the likes of Rooney and Ronaldo, and was at the centre of United's best attacking moves. However, when faced with a blue wall, the young attacking duo could not break through, ensuring a quiet afternoon for Petr Cech in the Chelsea goal. After the game Ferguson admitted fatigue had got the better of his players after their gruelling campaign.

'You can't do much about it when it comes so late,' Ferguson told the *Observer*. 'The players are too tired. I have seen it time and time again in football – the important thing is to accept it and get on with it. I will wake up in the morning and get on with my life.'

Scholes netted seven goals in the 2006–07 season, which was a good haul considering the new role he was being asked to play. However, moving back into the centre of midfield meant he had to put himself about more with regard to tackling, something he admits he struggles with – culminating in red cards against Liverpool and Roma in high-octane matches with the season reaching its climax.

A two-goal haul against Newcastle at St James' Park on New Year's Day had rescued United from the jaws of defeat against the Magpies, and had begun their never-say-die attitude, which eventually won them the title. Goals from Ronaldo and John O'Shea, when the game seemed dead and buried, picked up crucial points that eventually won them the title. Scholes had forged an understanding with midfield partner Michael Carrick, and, with two creative midfield players, there was plenty of service to the frontmen, with Ronaldo in particular the scourge of defences up and down the country. Ferguson knew full well that Scholes's game was about more than a solid right foot and late runs into the box, with his gradual move back into the centre of midfield changing his game to rely on the strength of his passing – which drew plaudits from teammates and opponents. At the age of 32 Scholes had proved justified in extending his career at Manchester United and could still be a major force at the club despite being in the twilight of his career. With young players such as Ronaldo and Rooney, Ferguson's team were evolving but were still reliant on the likes of Giggs and Scholes for experience when playing at the highest level.

To ensure that the gap over Chelsea should remain, United wasted no time in adding to their squad in the pre-season, raiding the Portuguese league for two of their brightest prospects. With Scholes and Giggs reaching the twilight of their careers, Ferguson went looking for the replacements, using the same contacts from assistant Carlos Queiroz as had seen them snare Cristiano Ronaldo four years previously. They snapped up another Sporting Lisbon youngster, Nani, who had been dubbed the new Ronaldo due to his quick feet, balance and agility.

Meanwhile, Brazilian midfielder Anderson, who had been on United's radar for some time, was taken from the champions, Porto. The pair came with a combined price tag of over £40 million, but the spending was not complete. The protracted transfer saga of England international Owen Hargreaves was finally put to rest when he inked a contract at Old Trafford following a £20 million move from Bundesliga heavyweights Bayern Munich.

A former foe also came to join the champions as Argentine Carlos Tévez, who had scored the only goal of the game on the last day of the season to spoil the end-of-season party at Old Trafford, joined on a loan deal from West Ham. The east London side had been hit with a heavy fine for breaching premier League rules in attaining the South American star, as he, along with Javier Mascherano, were owned by a third party. However,

United saw an opportunity to capitalise on the mêlée and secured a two-year loan deal for the combative forward, who had single-handedly staved off relegation for the Hammers the previous year.

Manchester United were a club that depended upon around evolution, and it was clear to see that Ferguson was eager to continue this by bringing in Europe's finest talent to learn from his established stars, before one day replacing them in the starting 11. Scholes and Giggs had perhaps two or three seasons left in them and Ferguson did not waste time with players who could dominate in the short term. He was continuing his legacy by building for the future.

After winning the season's curtain raiser against Chelsea in the Charity Shield, in which Scholes took no part, United began the defence of their title at home to Reading, who had been something of a bogey team for Ferguson's side since achieving their top-flight status. Scholes started in the centre of midfield alongside Michael Carrick, while only Nani was given his Premier League bow as a second-half substitute for Wayne Rooney. The Portuguese winger had more than a passing resemblance to his countryman Ronaldo, with slick skills confusing the Reading defenders, who now had to cope with pacey Portuguese threats on both flanks. However, he could not mark his debut with a goal, as former Red Steve Coppell led his compact side to a hard-earned goalless draw at the Theatre of Dreams. The Old Trafford faithful had expected to see United come bursting out of the blocks, sending out a message of intent as they had done with their 5–1 mauling of Fulham in the corresponding fixture last term; but they were to be found wanting against the Berkshire side. United heaped instant pressure on their title rivals with a blistering start to their previous campaign, and were eager to get back on track against Portsmouth, who had beaten them last year in a result that could have cost them the title.

The Portsmouth – or 'Pompey' – players spent more time goading Cristiano Ronaldo, and the Portuguese winger took the bait, earning a red card for a head butt as Harry Redknapp's side got their reward for their wind-up tactics. Scholes had given United the lead inside 15 minutes with a firmly hit strike that was an early contender for goal of the month, a typically sweet strike that left David James flapping at thin air as the net bulged behind him. However, the home side earned a draw with a second-half goal from Zimbabwean striker Benjani, to give United two points out of a possible six at the start of the season.

However, they would have been pleased to take a point from the Manchester derby at Eastlands as a solitary goal from Geovani maintained Sven-Göran Eriksson's 100 per cent start in his first season in charge at United's bitter rivals. The Brazilian struck on the half-hour mark and, despite the best efforts of the United players, they could not find an equaliser as City claimed the bragging rights over their local rivals.

United found themselves in unfamiliar territory without a win in their first three games, and the pain of losing the derby hit the United players deeply. However, there was the chance for retribution against Spurs at Old Trafford. Scholes and Carrick formed the midfield partnership in the early part of the season, with Giggs occupying the left flank. And, with Cristiano Ronaldo suspended, Nani was thrust into the limelight a lot earlier than Ferguson had intended. The Portuguese winger repaid a large chunk of his transfer fee with a stunning 25-yard strike to win the game for his new side.

Hargreaves, Nani and Tévez were joined by debutant Anderson as United fielded a much-changed side against Roy Keane's Sunderland. The United legend had taken the Wearsiders from the obscurity of the Championship to the Premier League at the first time of asking and would face his former club for the first time as a manager. Keane had set his side out to unnerve United's young charges, and Anderson in particular looked to struggle with the rigours of English football. However, with Scholes alongside him, the Brazilian grew into the game and was able to exert some influence.

An unconvincing United poached a one-goal victory through Louis Saha with less than 20 minutes remaining to make it two wins on the trot after their nightmare start.

Scholes next saw action against Everton at Goodison Park as United picked up another one-goal victory thanks to Nemanja Vidić's late header.

Manchester United's new signings were to be used sparingly by Ferguson in their first year in English football, with Anderson in particular able to learn off Scholes in the middle of the park – and there could be few better role models for the young Brazilian. So Scholes continued to be one of the first names on Sir Alex Ferguson's team sheet well into September, as United continued their resurgence in the Champions League, which began with a trip to Sporting Lisbon, pitting both Ronaldo and Nani against their former employers. United continued in a similar vein to their domestic form – and picked up a one-goal victory, inevitably, through Ronaldo. The Portuguese winger stooped to head home a fine winner on the hour mark, though chose not to celebrate in front of the fans who once idolised him.

In midweek, British football was rocked by the departure of José Mourinho from Chelsea, by mutual consent. The Portuguese tactician boasted a fine record against Sir Alex Ferguson and Manchester United, going back to his days at Porto, but relinquishing the league, coupled with boardroom strife, ensured the end of a great love affair in the capital. Mourinho was replaced by director of football Avram Grant whose first game in charge would prove to be at Old Trafford, and the match would prove to be a baptism of fire for the Israeli coach.

Grant was not a popular choice among Chelsea fans, who felt nobody could replace Mourinho, and their worst fears were realised when an anonymous Chelsea were comprehensively beaten at the Theatre of Dreams. Ferguson opted for a 4–4–2 against the former champions, who would employ a similar system favoured by Mourinho. Scholes and Carrick marshalled the midfield while Giggs and Ronaldo provided width, with Rooney and Tévez providing plenty of movement and running upfront. It was the Argentine who opened the scoring, planting a front-post header past Petr Cech on the stroke of half time after former United target John Obi Mikel had been sent off for a high challenge on Patrice Evra. The points were made safe in injury time, thanks to a Louis Saha penalty, as United claimed an early scalp in their quest to retain the title.

If there were any Chelsea fans wishing to be open-minded about the appointment of Grant, this convincing Manchester United victory settled the debate. Scholes, in his new, deep role, would pick the ball up from the back four and spray the ball forward to the likes of Rooney, Ronaldo and Tévez, who could terrorise defences with their movement and pace.

Proving the perfect protection for a rock-solid back four, Scholes helped United go eight games without conceding a goal in all competitions. The centre-back pairing of Vidić and Ferdinand were dominant, while Patrice Evra and Wes Brown provided ample cover and width on either side.

United edged past Birmingham City by a now familiar 1–0 scoreline before their crunch Champions League tie with Roma at Old Trafford. Eager not to suffer further humiliation at the Theatre of Dreams, Roma provided bullish opposition and, in Totti and Mancini, had more than enough talent to cause an upset at Old Trafford. However, the hosts were made of stronger stuff, and Wayne Rooney's 70th-minute goal settled the tie to maintain Ferguson's 100 per cent start to the campaign.

By October, United had got into the stride, buoyed by their return to form, and began to add flair and conviction to go with their guile throughout October. Scholes helped United to convincing wins over Wigan and Aston Villa as the goals began to flow for Sir Alex Ferguson's team. However, Scholes suffered a lengthy injury at the end of October that would keep him out for three months, including the critical Christmas period, when the games would come thick and fast for the champions.

The 3-1 victory over Spurs would be Scholes's last action of 2007, meaning Anderson and Nani would have to play much more than Ferguson had intended in their first season in England.

Scholes injured knee ligaments and required surgery, meaning a lengthy injury layoff over the winter. At first, club doctors estimated he would be out for 12 weeks after undergoing surgery in early November, but by the start of the New Year he was itching to get back into action. 'I have started running now,' Scholes told Manutd.com early in the new year. 'I have got these next few weeks to get as fit as I can so hopefully I will be fresh when I come back. It's a couple of months since the operation now and everything seems to be OK. I am on track to return at the end of January or beginning of February.'

Never one to sit back and watch his teammates struggle, Scholes admitted his impatience after another lengthy layoff. 'It has been frustrating for me. I still see all the games, but it gets a bit boring watching because all you want is to be out there playing – but in know that I have to be patient and hopefully I will be back playing soon.'

Ferguson, who rarely splashes out in the January transfer window, admitted that the return of Scholes was like signing a new player – and that he could go straight into the side for United's next game – an FA Cup tie with Spurs. 'He's a consideration because he's such a great player,' Ferguson said. 'He's champing at the bit, as you would expect with him. All week he's been begging the coaches for a game. We're very buoyed by having Paul come back. It's almost like a new signing at a very important time with Europe and the FA Cup starting.'

Scholes made a substitute appearance in the Old Trafford tie, coming off the bench to inspire United to a 3–1 victory over the north Londoners. Robbie Keane had fired Spurs ahead, only for Tévez to equalise seven minutes before the interval. Scholes replaced Carrick on 64 minutes, and it wasn't long before United took the lead, with Cristiano Ronaldo netting from the spot five minutes later, and the Portuguese winger secured United's safe passage with a second minutes from time.

'Something special seems to happen when the ball goes to [Scholes]', Ferguson said after the game. 'He has an innate sense of composure about him; the game just seems to stop so he controls it. He's an amazing player.'

Showing no ill effects after his return to the first team, Scholes started the next Premier League match against Portsmouth alongside Carrick, though he was replaced by Anderson on the hour mark as two Cristiano Ronaldo goals saw off Harry Redknapp's side. Moving into February, United continued to chase leaders Arsenal and would need to fend off their local rivals Spurs again if they were to keep in touch at the top of the league. Dimitar Berbatov, who has long been linked with a switch to Old Trafford, opened the scoring after 24 minutes, but Carlos Tévez was on hand to grab another crucial late goal to ensure that the spoils were shared.

The city of Manchester stood still on 6 February to mark the fiftieth anniversary of the Munich air disaster, in which eight United players lost their lives in Bavaria. Fittingly, the event would be marked at Old Trafford, with the opponents being Manchester City, on 10 February. Both sides wore special kits without names or sponsors in one of many tributes to those who had lost their lives. Much of the pre-match build-up had centred on the travelling Manchester City fans, and fears that they might ruin the minute's silence by whistling or jeering. But, to their credit, they did not disrupt the silence,. Scholes, in typically pragmatic fashion, insisted the United players must try to forget all the tension surrounding the match, and concentrate on getting three points in this crucial derby. Scholes partnered Anderson in the middle of the park, with Nani and Ronaldo and Giggs all starting. Ronaldo was moved upfront in an attempt to unsettle the City back four.

The semi-final with Barcelona pitted the two best footballing sides in the world against each other for a place in the Moscow showpiece. Barcelona were suffering indifferent league form and had all but surrendered La Liga to bitter rivals Real Madrid. There was much speculation about the future of manager Frank Rijkaard, with Champions League glory being touted as the only thing to save his job. Despite lying third in the league, Barcelona boasted Samuel Eto'o, Thierry Henry and Lionel Messi among their attacking options – with many expecting a blistering festival of attacking football between the two teams.

It was the first time Alex Ferguson and his side had returned to the stadium where they tasted success in the final of 1999 – but the Scot utilised an entirely different set of tactics against the much-lauded Catalans. As well as former Gunner Henry, Barça could call upon ex-Chelsea star Eidur Gudjohnsen for any insider information that could help stem the red tide. The Icelandic international told the *Daily Mirror* that, rather than

Rooney or Ronaldo, Scholes was the player they should pay most attention to. The game would be a showcase for some of the brightest young stars in world football with Rooney, Ronaldo, Anderson and Nani facing off against the likes of Messi and Bojan Krkić.

Gudjohnsen was well aware that United's elder statesman could pose a larger threat to their Champions League aspirations. 'It's not just about these two players,' he said. 'I am more of an admirer of Paul Scholes than I am of Ronaldo. Ronaldo is a fantastic player but he has ten other great players around him every week. Scholes is one of the most complete footballers I have ever seen.

'His one-touch play is phenomenal. Whenever I have played against him I never felt I could get close to him. Of course, players like Ronaldo or Messi can change a game with one bit of skill, but there is a lot of hysteria about them and the tie will be all about which of us plays better as a team. It will be a battle of two contrasting styles. We are good technically and, like most British teams, they are more physical. Both sides play great football.'

Meanwhile, United midfielder Michael Carrick stressed that the young side had learned from their semi-final capitulation at the hands of AC Milan at the same stage last year. 'It promises to be a great spectacle,' he told the *Guardian*. 'Everyone is talking about it because you dream about being involved on a night like this. Manchester United have not been to the Nou Camp for a while but the lads who were around in 1999 have spoken about what a special night it is. Last year we ended up a little bit thin and couldn't pull it off in Milan when it mattered but we now have enough bodies to cope with going for the title and the Champions League.

'It is the depth of the squad which has got us into this position. These games are won and lost on little details. We certainly have the players. It will be a test but I would like to think it will be more of a test for them.'

While Carrick said the older players had been sharing their experiences from their victory over Bayern Munich nine years ago, Ferguson urged his new side to write their *own* history. 'It's almost ten years ago now,' Ferguson said at a press conference. 'The team of today is the team of today and they don't need reminding about the past. They've seen it often enough on Manchester United TV, so I don't think it's lost on anyone. But I think what's even more important is that they can shape their own history and I think they're good enough to do that.'

The match would be a personal landmark for Scholes, who made his hundredth Champions League appearance for the club. Since making his debut over a decade before, Scholes had slowly drifted back to a deeper position, with late bursts into the area becoming more infrequent. Nowadays he could influence games from the middle of the park with his vision and passing. The match started at a frantic pace and an early foray into the Barcelona half brought instant rewards, as Gabriel Milito handled in the area to give Manchester United a penalty within the opening five minutes. The task fell to Cristiano Ronaldo, who had already amassed 38 goals during his incredible season. Amazingly the Portuguese master failed with the spot kick, sending the ball wide after sending Victor Valdés the wrong way.

The remainder of the match saw the United rearguard stifle any fledgling Barcelona attack, with the hosts forging very few clear-cut chances despite having the lion's share of possession. With the defence dealing so capably with Barça's plethora of attacking quality, Scholes was able to pick up the scraps and dictate the pace of the game, picking the ball off the back four.

'I thought he was one of our best players,' Ferguson said after the game. 'His reading of the play outside the box was terrific. His interceptions were marvellous and he never gave the ball away.'

Many were surprised by the defensive mindset employed by the visitors, but a goalless draw at the Nou Camp represented a good evening's work for Manchester United, who now needed only victory on home soil to book their place in the Champions League final.

Manchester United hosted Barcelona in the second leg of their Champions League semi-final on 29 April, with the noise and weight of expectation building to a crescendo inside Old Trafford. Frank Rijkaard knew a solitary goal would put them in the driving seat, with United needing to score more in order to go through. The game kicked off with the usual sparring between the two sides before Scholes stepped up with a moment of magic. The game was only 14 minutes old when the ball fell to him 20 yards from goal. Because he had not scored since August, and now occupied a deeper role, many had fallen into a false sense of security when the United midfielder had the ball in this sort of area. Scholes took the ball down and hit an instant right-foot shot, rolling back the years with a trademark long-range drive that flew past a helpless Victor Valdés before finding the top right-hand corner of the net. Old Trafford exploded as Scholes wheeled away to celebrate the goal that would send Manchester United through to only their third Champions League final.

Barcelona huffed and puffed, looking for an equaliser, with both sides missing gilt-edged chances before the referee blew the final whistle. A solitary Paul Scholes goal, only his second of the season, had sent Manchester United through to the first ever all-English Champions League final. Despite his match-winning heroics, Scholes could not be coaxed in front of a microphone to share in his moment of glory.

'He'll be the first name on my team sheet in the final,' Ferguson told ITV. 'He's one of the great players to come through the ranks here. It was a fantastic goal – I don't think we can expect Paul Scholes to score ten to fifteen goals a season as he did when he was younger. It was a marvellous moment for him. It makes up for all the goals he can't score now because of his age.'

With no suspension or injury to rule him out, Scholes was free to take his place on the grandest stage in club football, something he had so cruelly been denied nine years before.

'It was an awesome strike, we have seen him do it in training and a few times before,' Michael Carrick told the Associated Press. 'It has got to be one of his best, on a game like that and a night like that. It was something special. Once we are there, we believe we can win but it will be tough.'

Manchester United's captain, Rio Ferdinand, could not describe the joy of earning a place in his first Champions League final. 'You can't put it into words,' he said. The fans played their part and backed us the whole way and we dug in deep. Then there was a moment of quality from a fantastic player. Paul Scholes – what a goal! A great time to get one.'

United would discover their opponents the following night when Chelsea and Liverpool contested their semi-final second leg at Stamford Bridge. With Chelsea holding the advantage with an away goal, many expected a drab encounter. However, after a scintillating 120 minutes of football, the west London side emerged victorious, as Britain's top two would compete for the grandest prize in club football.

With the build-up to the final gathering pace, and the eyes of Europe turning to Moscow, Scholes drew praise from across the Continent from managers and players alike. Marcello Lippi, Italy's World Cup-winning coach, told the BBC sport website how highly he had always rated the Manchester United midfielder. 'Paul Scholes would have been one of my first choices for putting together a great team – that goes to show how highly I have always rated him. Scholes is a player I have always liked, because he combines great talent and technical ability with mobility, determination and a superb shot.

'He is an all-round midfielder who possesses character and quality in abundance. In my opinion, he has been one of the most important players for United under Sir Alex.'

While his role in the side may have changed, Lippi admits older players have the experience necessary to affect play from deep. 'With age, the best players learn to be effective in different areas of the pitch,' he continued. 'For example, Andrea Pirlo can play just in front of the defence, right in the middle, behind the strikers, he can play everywhere. The same goes for Scholes.'

In the same article, former Manchester United youth team coach Eric Harrison sang the praises of his former star. 'People always say Paul looks like he's got so much time,' he said. 'That's because his positional sense is second to none and he knows what's around him before he receives the ball. Paul has no great pace or power, but he makes up for that with his reading of the game, his awareness and his superb touch. The only current player who would come close to him in that regard is Cesc Fàbregas.'

Harrison recalled the youth-team days at Manchester United, when Scholes was a fans' favourite despite his tender years. 'We used to get big crowds turning up for our home games at The Cliff in those days. Word had got round about the fantastic group of players we had – David Beckham, Nicky Butt, Ryan Giggs and the Neville brothers. Yet the fans' favourite was always Scholes. People were amazed that this tiny ginger kid with asthma could smack a ball so hard, that he had such a fantastic touch and was so brave. And he has not gone on to do too bad after that.'

The one player who could better Scholes in terms of silverware in the Ferguson era called for his inclusion in the starting 11 in Moscow. Ryan Giggs claimed Scholes deserved a starting place over any other United players.

'I am not telling the manager who to pick,' he told *The Times*. 'But Scholesy deserves to play because he is a great player. His form has been brilliant and his goal against Barcelona got us to the final. To play with a player like him is a privilege. He does things other players can't do. The disappointment of 1999 was massive for him and Roy [Keane] having played such an important part in getting us to the final. I am glad he has got another chance now and he deserves it.'

Scholes told Sky Sports ahead of the encounter of his dismay at missing the 1999 showpiece. 'It was a good night really,' he said. 'The lads went out and won the game. I would have liked to have been involved but it wasn't to be. You don't really feel a part of it when you haven't played.'

But, despite promises from the manager that he would start, Scholes said he did not want a sympathy vote due to his having missed out nine years before. 'I want to be there on my merit,' he told the *Daily Mirror*. 'If I am not playing well, the manager is not going to say: "You missed the final ten years ago, go and play for ten minutes." I think whether you have missed a chance or not, it is a massive tournament for everybody involved, even players like Milan's Paulo Maldini who have won it five times.'

Former Busby Babe Wilf McGuinness, who took over from Sir Matt Busby as boss in 1969, believes Manchester United have reason to be grateful to Fergie's Fledglings, who remained with the club after the 1999 final, a side, he believes, that will take some matching. 'You had David Beckham on one side and Giggs on the other,' he explained in Liverpool's *Daily Post*. 'You couldn't ask for more than that. Ryan was a terrific player, along with some of the other players coming through at the same time. Paul Scholes, Gary Neville, Nicky Butt, Wes Brown – they have all come through really well. And now they have got that experience just to slow it down and not get too excited.

221

'Paul Scholes is another great player – as long as he doesn't tackle! It's great that they have grown up together. There is a bonding there and it brings back many memories for me of the Busby Babes. For Ryan to do it and for Paul Scholes to have a taste of it because he was suspended last time would be fantastic, he said of Manchester United's chances of glory. 'I think they'll do it.'

Ole Gunnar Solskjaer, who scored the winning goal in Barcelona to end the challenge of Bayern Munich nine years before, told the same newspaper of his desire to see Scholes experience action in the Champions League final after so cruelly being denied it in 1999. 'He has never complained about it,' he said. 'Not once. He just gets his head down and gets on with it. I get reminded all the time about that game – I get so many people coming up to me and giving me the thumbs-up. It was the greatest night of my life – but don't tell my wife that!

'He [Scholes] is a model professional. We used to have bets on who would come out for training first, but there is no point any more because it is always Scholes. He is always the first one out because he loves being here. He is such a great player to have in the team; I really enjoyed playing with him over the years. He always gives a good performance in midfield, he gets in the box, he scores goals and he is a winner. He always wants to win. Every single training session – when I am refereeing and I make a bad decision he lets me know about it!'

Manchester United had a massive psychological edge over Chelsea after pipping Avram Grant's side to the Premier League title – a fact Argentinian forward Carlos Tévez believed would haunt the west Londoners. 'We are better than Chelsea', he told *The Times*. 'That is a psychological problem for them. They may say the Premier League is another story, another issue, but we are convinced that it will have an impact on what happens in the final.

'We are favourites and everyone knows it. We are not worried by Chelsea, we are concentrated and focused – but for them it is different. This is more than a final for them. Their whole season rests on the outcome of this final and I am convinced that they have some problems in their team. We have no extra pressure. We are under pressure every game and we feel an obligation to win every time we play. The manager is very happy that we won the league, we know how seriously he wants to win the Champions League again.'

Even for Manchester United's crop of global stars, the fiftieth anniversary of the Munich air disaster was not lost – with the sense of occasion adding extra motivation for every team member. It shows the sense of community and shared passion for Manchester United that South Americans and Asians share the same sense of responsibility as the home-grown Manchester boys.

'We all agree that it would be fantastic if we can commemorate what happened by winning a trophy and dedicating it to those people that died', Tévez continued. 'Sir Bobby Charlton told me how much he wanted us to win the Champions League and what it would mean to him. He was emotional and so was I.'

Ahead of the game many felt Manchester United had fate on their side, with too many forces at work that would make defeat at the hands of Chelsea impossible. In 1999 the Champions

League was won on the ninetieth birthday of Sir Matt Busby; in 2008 the club were celebrating the lives of fantastic young footballers who so tragically lost their lives in the only way they knew how: by winning silverware.

The recent troubles at the UEFA Cup final, played at the City of Manchester Stadium, had caused a media furore regarding security in Moscow, as the Reds and the Blues would meet on foreign soil, where English football fans rarely excel. The Russian police had promised to be firm with any fan trouble – for once, the football was not the only talking point in the Champions League final. For Scholes the game would be the chance to banish the ghosts of 1999, and he intended to relish every moment of his first appearance in the world's top club match.

'It doesn't matter what anyone else says', he told Sky Sports. 'You know yourself that you haven't played in the game that has won the trophy. If I had played, we might not have won the game. You just don't know – it could happen like that. On the night I was really pleased – glad the lads played as they did and managed to win the game for us – but I wasn't a part of that and you've got to live with it.'

With much of the pre-match talk focused on the fiftieth anniversary of the Munich air crash, and with the final falling forty years after the Busby Babes claimed European glory, Ferguson admitted his side were out to shape their own history in Moscow. 'Our history is an illustrious history', he said in a pre-match press conference. 'But there's a weakness in terms of European trophies we've won and I hope that we can go some way to making that better tomorrow night.'

After all the pre-match tension, there was little or no fan trouble in Moscow as the stringent Russian security cast a looming shadow on proceedings, while fear of the unknown forced immediate good behaviour on the intimidated fans from London and Manchester. The teams filed out onto the pitch past the giant trophy, ready to do battle for the grandest prize in club football. This was Chelsea's first Champions League final, a feat achieved by much-maligned boss Avram Grant – going one step further than his predecessor, José Mourinho. Chelsea, too, were under immense pressure with the game being staged in the hometown of their Russian billionaire owner Roman Abramovich, who had funded the Blue Revolution at Chelsea and turned them into a dominant force in English football.

Scholes lined up alongside Michael Carrick in the middle of the park along with Owen Hargreaves, whose stamina and athleticism would prove crucial in wearing down Chelsea's powerhouse midfield. United opted for three frontmen with Rooney, Ronaldo and Tévez all fluid and interchangeable – meaning Chelsea's defenders would face a constant headache. The final started tentatively, with both sides engaged in early sparring, testing out the Luzhniki pitch, which had met with criticism from the British media.

Ferguson's side began to dominate and took the lead through Cristiano Ronaldo, who escaped the attentions of marker Michael Essien to power a superb header past the stranded Petr Cech. Ronaldo had proved wrong the few doubters he had: he had delivered on the biggest stage of them all. Chelsea would now have to come out of their shell and attack, which would leave them vulnerable to the counterattack, where Manchester United excelled. Scholes faced a difficult battle in the centre of the park against France legend Claude Makelele, who epitomised everything a world-class defensive midfielder should be. He can read the game superbly, is strong in the tackle and rarely loses possession.

The two were chasing a 50–50 ball soon after the goal when Scholes was caught in the face, with the two players instantly going to ground with head wounds. Blood gushed down Scholes's face, as his nose had been broken from the force of the collision. After the euphoria of taking the lead, Scholes feared he may not make it until half time after such a long wait to appear in a Champions League final. However, it would take more than that to keep the midfielder down, and he bravely continued despite the agony of the injury.

Makelele, too, brushed himself off and the two were able to continue. United continued to press and could have doubled their lead, with Tévez denied at close range by Cech, who leapt up to deny Michael Carrick, who had followed up with an instant strike, which the Czech international did superbly to turn away. The Argentine striker then found himself inches from sliding in a second as Chelsea survived.

As happens so often in football, United were made to pay for failing to take their chances as Chelsea equalised on the stroke of half time. Essien, who had been run ragged by Ronaldo the entire half, hit a speculative 30-yard drive that deflected off both Rio Ferdinand and Nemanja Vidić before falling at the feet of Frank Lampard, who capitalised on a slip from Van der Sar to slot home an unlikely equaliser.

Ferguson's half-time team talk had been made that much harder as the wind was well and truly knocked out of their sails and Chelsea came out much stronger in the second half. The Blues began to dominate the midfield, with German captain Michael Ballack pulling the strings in midfield, feeding the dangerous Ivorian Didier Drogba, who would not give the United defence a minute's peace.

Hearts were in United mouths when Drogba tried his luck from range – the ball had the beating of Van der Sar, but came back off the post with the Dutch keeper scrambling across goal. Scholes had struggled in the second period with injury hampering his performance. Ferguson withdrew the midfielder and, shortly before the end with extra time looming, brought on Ryan Giggs, who made his 759th performance in a United shirt, breaking Bobby Charlton's appearance record, which had stood for more than thirty years.

The Welshman came within inches of stealing victory for Manchester United when he prodded the ball towards goal with Cech hopelessly out of position. The ball seemed destined for the back of the net before captain John Terry adjusted his body to flick the ball over the crossbar with his head – ensuring extra time was needed to separate England's top two. Both sides began to tire as the Moscow rain became heavier and more persistent, but it was Chelsea who carved out the better opening, with Frank Lampard again afforded room in the area, but he could only scoop the ball onto the crossbar with Van der Sar a mere spectator once again.

The thirty-minute period of extra time expired with neither

side able to find a winner, which meant the 2008 Champions league final would be decided by a penalty shoot-out – a lottery. The shoot-out took place in front of the United end of the stadium, with their team taking the first shot towards glory. Both sides found the back of the net with their first two penalties before Cristiano Ronaldo, whose 42 goals had propelled United for much of the season, had his tame penalty beaten away by Petr Cech.

Chelsea dispatched their next penalty, which gave Chelsea skipper John Terry the chance to win the Champions League, should he beat Van der Sar with his next kick. The Dutchman, who already had a Champions League winner's medal with Ajax, bounced around in nervous anticipation on the touchline as Terry paced backwards. Incredibly, the Chelsea skipper slipped before making contact with the ball, on the very patch of grass on which Van der Sar had slipped to allow Frank Lampard a near open goal to equalise.

Despite sending the goalkeeper the wrong way, Terry could only hit the upright as United lived to fight another day. After securing their next spot kick the responsibility fell to Nicolas Anelka, a £15 million signing from Bolton Wanderers in the January transfer window. Anelka had been playing out of position for much of his time at Stamford Bridge and looked uncomfortable making the long walk from the halfway line to the penalty area. The Frenchman's spot kick was firm, but Van der Sar guessed the right way and beat away his effort, crowning Manchester United Kings of Europe for the third time in their history.

The United players ran forward to celebrate with their goalkeeping hero – with Ronaldo sinking to the floor in tearful jubilation. The Portuguese winger had been spared.

'When we missed the penalty kick we thought we were in trouble,' Ferguson told Sky Sports with the post-match euphoria erupting in the Luzhniki stadium. 'But I think we deserved it. We had the best chances. In the second half they had a lot of control but in extra time we were much better. It's a great team a fantastic achievement.'

But Ferguson told the Associated Press after the game how Scholes had now banished his Champions League final ghosts: 'The disappointment of '99 has now gone for him,' said the Scot. 'He was very groggy at half time and we had to give him some tablets but I am delighted for the boy – he is a fantastic person. People like Scholes, Ryan Giggs, Gary Neville know what Manchester United means. Scholes and Giggs will contribute next season, if not as many games.'

Ferguson admitted that European history had played into their hands on the night. 'We had a cause, which is very important,' he told the *Belfast Times*. 'People with causes are difficult to battle against and I think fate was playing its part.'

Victory in Moscow proved Ferguson could be more than a one-season wonder in Europe. The Scot had built another young side that stood at the summit of British and European football and could go on to dominate the footballing world for years to come. Scholes was part of the first batch of Fergie's Fledglings, who rose through the ranks at Old Trafford and guided the club to the most successful season in over a hundred years of history. Now

Scholes is well into his thirties, his experience has proved crucial in helping to nurture a new crop of young talent to take Manchester United forward.

Chapter 9

ENGLAND INTERNATIONAL

'I played with Paul since we were 15 and he is one of
his country's best ever players.'
DAVID BECKHAM

Paul Scholes won 66 caps for England and netted 14 goals,
playing in two World Cups and two European Championships,
tasting bitter defeat as England's hunt for glory was cut short at
every turn.

The Manchester United youngsters who had begun to
establish themselves as permanent fixtures in Ferguson's first
team in the 1996–97 season had pushed for a place in the
national side, and former Spurs great Glenn Hoddle gave Scholes
his international bow against South Africa in a match – staged,
fittingly, at Old Trafford – on 24 May 1997.

One of Scholes's fellow fledglings, Phil Neville, was afforded a
starting place alongside Martin Keown, Stuart Pearce and Gareth
Southgate in an experienced England backline, while Teddy

Sheringham and Ian Wright would look to fill the void left by Alan Shearer in attack.

For Scholes the match proved how far he had come from the streets of Middleton, as his performances for the biggest club in England justified a place in Hoddle's plans as the race for the World Cup in France intensified. There was an electric atmosphere at Old Trafford, serving as early proof of the benefits of staging England internationals across the country, rather than having them centralised in London. This would later be adopted when the Three Lions were temporarily homeless, following the demolition of the old Wembley and the building of the £750 million monolith that now stands on the site.

Newcastle United's Rob Lee put England in front after a telling delivery from Sheringham before Phil Masinga equalised for the visitors. With qualification for the 1998 World Cup less than secure, a draw against the unfancied South Africans would have done little to enhance England's billing as potential winners following a strong showing at Euro '96. So, after 64 minutes, Sheringham was withdrawn and replaced by Scholes to play behind Wright in a position in which he was often utilised at club level. The move paid dividends, as Scholes intelligently flicked Paul Gascoigne's free kick into the path of Wright, who calmly finished to secure an unconvincing 2–1 victory for the Three Lions.

While injuries to Jamie Redknapp and Gascoigne overshadowed the friendly, manager Hoddle praised Scholes after his international bow. 'He's got a bright future,' he said. 'He showed a lot of maturity, and it was a lovely little flick for the Wright goal.

'There's a bright future for these United players,' he continued. 'They all have talent, and, when they're twenty-four or twenty-five years old, they'll have heads of twenty-nine- thirty-year-olds, because of the experience they are getting in the Champions League and in international football.'

Hoddle also praised the nurturing of the young stars at Manchester United, as the experience of playing for England's top club had given them maturity beyond their tender years for which the England boss was eternally grateful.

'This is something we have lacked,' he admitted. 'When Liverpool had their super, super side, they were all men who were mature players – and not many of them were English. Scholes did well – he showed a lot of maturity.'

Scholes's teammate, Gary Neville, said he was far from surprised that he so comfortably made the transition to international level, because of the planning and preparation of the Manchester United coaching staff. 'Scholes did brilliantly when he made his England debut,' he said. 'But I always thought he would. It's nothing to do with experience: it's all about temperament.

'We've got a head start,' Neville confessed. 'Playing at United, you can be on the scrapheap very quickly, but, if you get in, eventually the rewards are massive.'

Despite this, Scholes did not merit a place in the England side in their next qualifying game, against Poland, but earned a place in the four-team Tournoi, which served as a prelude to the following summer's tournament and pitted the Three Lions against World Cup hosts France, 1994 runners-up Italy and holders Brazil.

However, despite the snub for a difficult trip to Poland, Scholes never left Hoddle's plans following his first appearance in an England shirt, and the national coach said he was in no doubt of the United midfielder's potential after his first day with the England squad.

'When we met up at Mottram Hall before the South Africa game at Old Trafford, I saw enough on the first day's training to suggest that Paul has immense talent', he said. 'He's a mature player for his age. He can play off the front men, he can play in central midfield or out wide. He's very clever on the ball, he's got good feet and good vision, he can finish and he makes runs beyond the ball.'

Scholes was given his full debut in the opening match against Italy in Nantes on Wednesday, 4 June 1997, a game that would serve as the dress rehearsal for the crucial World Cup qualifier in Rome, which would take place in October.

'It's an exciting opportunity for young players to play against the best', Hoddle said of Le Tournoi. 'I might come away thinking, "He couldn't adapt" or "He did much better than I thought he would." ' The tournament would certainly not be taken lightly by France or Brazil, who, as hosts and holders respectively, did not have to qualify for the tournament and would need competitive action ahead of the finals in a year's time.

The match against Italy, like his debut for Manchester United, went superbly for Scholes, who set up Ian Wright to break the deadlock and got on the scoresheet himself with a left-footed volley on the stroke of half time to give Hoddle's side a 2–0 win over the Italians. And Hoddle admitted he was pleased with Scholes's performance in a game that would give England a massive psychological edge over their rivals. 'I didn't put any pressure on the boy,' he said. 'But you always give youngsters their head, and he's taken his opportunity well.

'He had an excellent game and showed a great deal of maturity,' Hoddle continued. 'He's a creative midfield player with the ability to score goals. I was very pleased with the way he played.'

At the tender age of 22, Scholes had once again proved he was destined for the grandest arenas that the beautiful game can offer, and confessed his delight at scoring on his full debut. 'That's got to be the greatest goal of my career,' he said. 'The feeling when it went into the net was unbelievable.'

Hoddle continued to lavish praise on the young midfielder, drawing comparisons with the France legend Michel Platini, and he believed Scholes's performance was all the more impressive due to the short amount of time the players had to train together.

'Against Italy in Nantes we played a different system with Scholes and Teddy Sheringham getting into the box from deeper positions,' he explained. 'We only had a couple of days to work on this, which tells you that the lad has an astute mind and a good footballing brain to be able to pick it up so quickly. The ball he hit for Wright was a Platini ball, wasn't it?'

The performance was not lost on club manager Alex Ferguson, who gave assurances that Scholes was now ready to establish himself as a regular fixture in the Manchester United side.

'Paul will be a first-team player next season,' he said. 'He's a first-team player now. We knew from his days in the youth team that he would be one of the best.' The Scot even admitted he had to fend off interest from other clubs looking to take Scholes away from Old Trafford. 'I've had several managers onto me about his availability', Ferguson confirmed. 'But there was never a chance of him leaving. His performance was absolutely brilliant and no surprise to me at all.'

The next match in Le Tournoi pitted England against World Cup hosts France, who had been undone by a moment of Roberto Carlos magic in their opening match with Brazil. Goalkeeper Fabien Barthez stood a helpless spectator as the Brazilian's left-footed drive swerved around the wall and nestled inside the left-hand post.

Eager not to fail ahead of the staging football's grandest party, France would be eager to win, and Hoddle admitted that Scholes now posed a dilemma. 'I need to see if he can reproduce what he showed me on Wednesday,' he said. 'He hit me between the eyes with what he did and I need to find out a little bit more about his temperament and whether he can play like that in the long term. If he can, then I might think, "Yes we've got a player on our hands here." But if he can't then it's not a disaster. I don't want to put pressure on the boy.'

Alan Shearer echoed his manager's sentiments, insisting the media must not bring too much expectation on the young prodigy. 'He's only got two caps so we mustn't build him up to be a world beater,' said the Geordie. 'I would imagine the media have been buffing us up at home, so we mustn't get carried away.

'I was delighted for him,' Shearer said of Scholes's first international goal. 'He's had trouble breaking into the Manchester United side, let alone England. Had it not been for Eric Cantona, he would have been a regular.'

bagged the second as England cruised to a 2–0 victory against the indomitable Lions.

Clutching a bottle of champagne after Scholes's match-winning display, the England boss said the player had once again withdrawn from the limelight once the final whistle had blown. 'He's such a level-headed boy, he was embarrassed about receiving it,' Hoddle said.

'I'm delighted for the lad. I wanted to pick him some time ago because we could all see the talent he has, but it was difficult because he was not playing regularly for Manchester United. Now he's come in and proved he can score at international level. It was a fantastic finish. He's a boy with a lovely mentality and temperament.'

Scholes himself said he was delighted with his early form for club and country, especially after netting on his birthday. 'You couldn't get a better birthday present,' he said. 'Anyone who's got three in five games has got to be happy with that.'

While the plaudits drew blushes from Scholes, he was aware that he could not show the same front on the pitch, but, typically, he believed there was still plenty of room for improvement.

'I got a bit sloppy towards the end. I was giving the ball away a bit more than I should have done, and the goal made things better for me. You have to feel confident when you go out there. There's no point in staying in your shell. You've got to express yourself as much as you can – and I believe the more I play at this level the more confident I'll become.'

With captain and talisman Alan Shearer a doubt for the finals, Scholes hoped the performance would prove him worthy of a place in Hoddle's final squad of 22. 'I don't think it'll do me any harm,' he said. 'There are six or seven of us trying to impress the boss, so competition is fierce.'

England duties were put to one side until the New Year and Scholes's first taste of international football in 1998 came in a friendly against Portugal in April, less than two months before the start of the tournament. A difficult season at club level ensured a subdued performance by Scholes – in for the injured Paul Gascoigne – but England still proved too strong for the Portuguese, cruising to a 3–0 victory at Wembley. And the World Cup warm-up was completed with a goalless draw against Saudi Arabia, in which Scholes again was afforded a starting place.

Despite having only seven international caps, Hoddle showed faith in the young United midfielder, and shocked many when he axed Paul Gascoigne from the final World Cup squad. Hoddle stuck by his decision, and was confident Scholes would not be overawed by the occasion. 'Nothing fazes Paul Scholes,' he told the *Independent*. 'I am sure he will play a big part in this World Cup – and I hope it is a big part.'

There was a media furore regarding the omission of Paul Gascoigne, and it thrust Scholes firmly into the spotlight, which he met with a typically bullish response. 'I am not Gazza number two. I am Paul Scholes number one,' he said. 'I'm not following anybody. I'll try to do it my way. What I believe, what I've been brought up to believe at Manchester United, is that if you have the talent it will come through. Perhaps it helps that I'm used to playing in big games with my club, but I honestly can't say I've been worried by anything so far in my career, either playing against top teams like Italy or following in the footsteps of Paul Gascoigne.'

Scholes, meanwhile, insisted he was a firm admirer of Gazza, and hoped to live up to the standards set by the Geordie. 'I've heard people say I can take Gazza's place but I try not to take too much notice,' he said. 'If I play I just want to play the way I play. Watching Gazza in 1990 is probably my biggest memory. It's the way he played, the way he beat people and the impact he had at that World Cup, it was sheer entertainment. I'm just a shy lad. It's the way I want to be – quite low-profile. I don't want to try to be somebody I'm not. I'm just a shy lad. I let Ryan Giggs and David Beckham get all the attention.'

If being touted as the new Paul Gascoigne affected Scholes, then he didn't show it on the pitch as he opened his World Cup account in the opening group game against Tunisia with a beautiful curling effort. 'People ask me if I was feeling any pressure after replacing Paul Gascoigne and I didn't feel a bit like that,' he admitted. 'I felt I had to produce and maybe make or score a goal, which I did. I had a few butterflies before the game but once I got out on to the pitch I felt fine – and then it's a question of trying to do your stuff.'

Despite taking the plaudits for the victory, Scholes confessed that the performance did not justify his inclusion in the squad at the expense of Gazza. 'I don't feel as if a weight has been lifted from my shoulders,' he said. 'It is, after all, only the first game. There's a long way to go and I've got to reproduce that kind of form in all the games to come. I was very happy when one did go in. I've had some highlights in my career but this has to be the highlight of all. I just hope I can go on and get a few more goals in the tournament.'

Fellow goalscorer and England captain Alan Shearer was delighted that Scholes justified Glenn Hoddle's faith. 'He scored from the most difficult chance,' he said. 'On another day he might have had a hat-trick. He's a tremendous little player with real quality. If he needed to prove anything, he did it today. People are looking at him to fill Paul Gascoigne's boots and, if this was a test, he came through with flying colours.'

Hoddle kept faith with Scholes in England's next group game against Romania a week later, which meant the Three Lions had to get something out of a powerful Colombian side on 26 June. David Beckham's glorious free kick was the outstanding moment of a 2–0 victory over the South Americans, which set up a clash against Argentina in the first knockout stage. Every time England face Argentina, political and sporting tensions make for a fantastic spectacle, and the match in St Etienne proved to be no different. Before the match, Scholes claimed he would have no qualms emulating Diego Maradona's 'hand of God' if it secured victory for the old enemy, as in the 1986 World Cup.

'I did get asked if I would do something similar to Maradona,' he explained. 'And, if it gets England through to the next round, the answer would be yes! I remember watching the game on television at home and when the ball went into the net I didn't think at first that Maradona had used his hand. When the television replays showed he *had* used his hand, like any England supporter I was very upset. The referee didn't see the goal, but that's in the past. We have to look to the future and go out and beat them.'

Before the Argentina game Scholes was chosen by the French newspaper *L'Équipe* as one of the best players in the tournament, and was afforded a place in their World XI – but he batted off the plaudits and instead chose to highlight where he had not featured so prominently. 'I was pleased with my first game, but not with my second,' he said. 'I didn't really have a chance or a shot, but I had a couple of shots against Colombia and felt I was in the game a bit more.'

The game was a typically open, fiery affair with the both sides creating good opportunities. Michael Owen announced himself on the world stage with a magnificent run and finish to give England the lead. But with the game deadlocked at 2–2, Beckham flicked a petulant boot at Argentina's Diego Simeone, who went to ground ensuring a straight red for the England number seven. England crashed out of the tournament on penalties as David Batty and Paul Ince failed to convert from the spot.

II

With England's pride battered following defeat by Argentina, there was no respite as qualification for the European Championships, due to be hosted by Holland and Belgium, began in September 1998, with the finals less than two years away. England were pitted against Sweden, Poland, Bulgaria and Luxembourg in a tricky group that made qualification less than a certainty. And it was not a triumphant return to the international scene for Scholes, as England lost their opening game 2–1 against Sweden, which was followed by a disappointing home draw with Bulgaria in October in which Scholes was replaced by Teddy Sheringham with a quarter of an hour remaining.

Despite the group phase being in its infancy, England's disastrous start to the campaign meant victory against minnows Luxembourg four days after was crucial to save their ailing campaign. The England support were baying for blood, but the 3–0 scoreline did little to satisfy the travelling fans.

England's hopes of making the finals were rocked further by Glenn Hoddle's announcement that he would be leaving his post with the national side. There had been plenty of heat on the former Spurs legend following a bizarre slur on the disabled culminating in his decision to quit. Hoddle was the man who had taken a punt on Scholes and given him his international bow – despite his not being a regular with Manchester United – but Howard Wilkinson would take charge of the national side for a home friendly with France in February 1999. Scholes was a late replacement for Jamie Redknapp in a 2–0 defeat, the first time France had ever beaten England on home soil.

Wilkinson's temporary spell as England boss was short-lived and Kevin Keegan was brought in as his replacement. Keegan had won admirers throughout the domestic game with his cavalier approach at Newcastle United, who had looked set to take the title away from Old Trafford before an end-of-season slump that saw them finish empty-handed. Qualification continued with the visit of Poland to Wembley in March in

Keegan's first game in charge and – as if it were needed – Scholes underlined his importance to the new regime. England won the game with a morale-boosting 3–1 victory and Scholes helped himself to a hat-trick, becoming the first England player since Ian Wright in 1993 World Cup final to bag three goals in the same game in an England shirt.

Scholes won the plaudits again as his country's saviour as the match-winning performance helped England get their campaign back on track. Scholes, however, admitted that the goals did not erase a painful miss against Argentina back in St Etienne the previous year.

'If I'd scored, England would have been 3–1 up and probably qualified,' he recalled after missing a gilt-edged opportunity to put the game beyond Argentina. 'I often think about it, I often replay it in my mind. The hat-trick doesn't wipe out the memory. The first goal was a touch of fortune, a lucky break. I can't remember too much about the second or where it came off me – I think it was my arm. The third goal was the best of all. Alan Shearer knocked the ball on and it was probably the best team goal.

'People will try to give me the glory but it was a team game,' he told the *People* afterwards. 'The team didn't feel pressure even though we knew the result was crucial. You have to hand it to Kevin Keegan, he has a way about him and is good at helping players relax and take their mind off the pressure.'

While Scholes was keen to share the plaudits, Keegan lavished praise on the United midfielder, insisting he should be honoured for his performance. 'He was magnificent,' Keegan told the *Mail on Sunday*. 'They usually knight you if you score a hat-trick here.

It should be Sir Paul Scholes! Don't forget he was playing in midfield today, he definitely deserved his man-of-the-match award.' Keegan also revealed that Scholes was reluctant to receive his man-of-the-match award, as it would mean he would have to face the media, something he is always loath to do.

'I don't often talk and I don't enjoy giving interviews,' Scholes said by way of confirmation to the press. 'Gary Neville has taken the match ball for me. I'm trying to carry the rest of the stuff!' The 77,000 crowd gathered at Wembley gave Scholes a standing ovation after he was replaced by Jamie Redknapp with less than ten minutes remaining. 'It's the best feeling I have had in football,' Scholes told the Associated Press. 'I have scored a few important goals for United in the Champions League but nothing like that. The crowd made me feel great when I came off; I have never felt anything like it before.'

England's next visitors were Sweden in June, their main rivals for top spot in the group. The Scandinavians had the upper hand after the opening group game in Stockholm, but, in front of a packed Wembley on 6 June 1999, the Three Lions were hopeful of restoring some pride. Keegan was afforded the rare luxury of a full complement of players and Scholes was rewarded with a more advanced midfield role with David Batty providing the anchor. England needed a win to keep alive their hopes of automatic qualification but, playing away from home, Sweden set their stall out to defend, and offered little in the final third of the pitch. Scholes picked up a caution on 27 minutes, which ensured he would miss the next game against Bulgaria, but a second booking just five minutes after the restart took England down to ten men. Two innocuous challenges afforded Scholes the unwanted title of the only England player to be sent off at Wembley as England's quest lay in tatters. The match finished goalless and meant England had to win their remaining three matches to stand any chance of making the finals.

'I am not the best tackler in the world, am I?' Scholes confessed in the *Mail on Sunday* later in the summer. 'It's probably because I started off as a forward. I haven't got the timing quite right but I don't go out deliberately hurting people. To be sent off at Wembley hurt me though. It's bound to. But it's now forgotten because I can't walk back in time and change it. I only wish I could.'

Scholes had enjoyed a honeymoon start to his England career, and admitted going through a rollercoaster of emotions playing for his country. 'I had such a fantastic high with the hat-trick against Poland – then that crushing low after Sweden. It's all my fault I know and I have no doubt about that,' he continued in a rare insight into his thoughts. 'It was such a disappointment and, believe me, it was a long walk to the Wembley tunnel. It took me ages to get there, seemed to last a lifetime in fact. It took me a few days to get over it because the papers were full of my dismissal. It filled the papers that weekend. I tried not to take too much notice then Kevin Keegan rang. He just repeated the advice of the afternoon before just to ignore all the fuss. Just forget it, he told me.

'Despite the papers, he was the only one I took notice of at the time. I had been sitting there worrying, though, wondering exactly what the England boss thought of me and what I had done. So that call from him was very welcome.'

Scholes admits that, although missing crucial games in the business end of England's qualification would be a burden, he was happy to assist when needed. 'I know sitting in the stands at Wembley will be tough enough but if I can help in Poland, from the bench or whatever, that's fine by me. I know we have to win these games to have any chance of qualifying.'

England travelled to Bulgaria four days later knowing another defeat would spell disaster for their bid. Jamie Redknapp replaced Scholes in the middle of the park and England could manage only a 1–1 draw in Sofia. A resounding 6–0 victory over the group whipping boys Luxembourg in September gave the Three Lions a timely morale boost – although the hapless visitors could boast only one full-time professional among their ranks. Scholes had now served his international suspension and was available for the trip to Poland four days later.

Keegan kept faith with the Manchester United star, as Scholes returned to the starting line-up against Poland in Warsaw. England struggled in the hostile Legia Stadium and were forced to settle for a goalless draw, which meant Sweden had to take points from Poland to secure second spot in the group for Kevin Keegan's side. Scholes went down in the penalty area under a heavy challenge from Tomasz Hajto – but the referee waved away the appeals. This time the Swedes came to the aid of the Three Lions, giving England a lifeline to secure a place at Euro 2000.

The playoff lottery pitted England against Scotland in an intriguing tussle for a place in the finals. Emotions would be running high during the home nations derby, and Scholes was eager to stress that the red mist would not descend during the two-legged match.

'On that occasion I was running around like a headless chicken most of the time,' Scholes said of his sending-off against Sweden. 'Maybe I was too hyped up. Maybe it was a case of me thinking I had to produce something again after my hat-trick against Poland and I was trying to do too much.'

Eager to live up to the aura he had created with his rich vein of form at the start of his international career, Scholes began to admit that the pressure weighed heavily on his shoulders. 'I've learned my lesson from that match,' he continued. 'I'll still go in tackling against the Scots but if I mistime one and get booked I will have to be more careful.'

If the pressure did have an effect on Scholes, it was put from his mind in the first leg of the playoff at Scotland's Hampden Park Stadium in mid-November 1999. He netted both goals as England gained a crucial advantage with a 2–0 victory. Buoyed by the showing, coach Kevin Keegan praised the Manchester United midfielder for his impact in what had been a roller-coaster ride in an England shirt. 'He doesn't talk a lot, but with him actions speak louder than words,' he told the Associated Press. 'The little fellow is a wonderful player. Sometimes it may seem he gets lost at Manchester United on the outside but in the dressing room they see him as a key player, and so do I.'

Scholes was pleased that England's attacking instincts paid dividends in Glasgow. 'I love getting forward,' he said. 'That's what the coach wants me to do and that's what I did today.'

The Hampden Park brace would have given Scholes great confidence ahead of the busy Christmas period for Manchester United, but he admitted that his prime concern was avoiding the wrath of Sir Alex Ferguson, for knocking the manager's nation out of the competition.

'I think Sir Alex will be pleased for me but more disappointed for Scotland,' Scholes told the *Daily Mail*. 'He wants the United boys to do well but I know he wanted Scotland to win more. Before the game he wouldn't tell me anything about the Scotland players so I didn't have an advantage, but deep down I am sure he will be proud of me.' And he confessed that thoughts of a second hat-trick had begun to creep in with England in full control of the match. 'It crossed my mind during the game that I could be on for a hat-trick,' he said. 'The most important thing is that we have a good result that we can take back to Wembley.'

The weight of expectation was lifted when Scholes netted the first, which led to some overexuberant celebrations, culminating in another booking. 'It was a silly thing to do when I look back on it,' he said. 'I should have restrained myself – I couldn't.'

With England in the driving set for qualification, Scholes was eager to stake his country's claim for silverware, admitting the side need to add to their trophy cabinet. 'There is a void in terms of England not having won a lot for a while,' he is quoted as saying in the *Western Daily Press*, 'whereas a lot of the lads in the club have tasted a lot of success. We are not taking anything for granted against Scotland. It's only half time and there is still a long way to go in the tie. We have to reproduce the same sort of performance in Wembley.'

The longstanding row of club versus country is irrelevant, according to Scholes, as footballers give their all when on the pitch regardless of the circumstances. 'It's not true to say that players don't feel as much for their country as they do for their club,' he said. 'Everyone give 100 per cent when they go out and play for England. It meant a lot to everyone to do the business against Scotland and when the first goal went in it meant the world to me. But rest assured: it means a lot to us against everybody. We always want to win.'

The second leg at Wembley took place four days later and a 1–0 victory gave Scotland their first win south of the border for 18 years, but it was not enough to send the tie into extra time as England held on for a 2–1 aggregate victory to book their place at Euro 2000. Don Hutchinson netted on 39 minutes while England failed to register a shot on target. Scholes was replaced by Ray Parlour in the dying seconds, but had more than played his part in securing England safe passage to Holland and Belgium in the New Year.

Ahead of the finals, United manager Sir Alex Ferguson heaped praise on Scholes, insisting he should be one of the first names on the England team sheet each time they play. 'Scholes is simply the best Englishman for the position he plays in – the best midfielder in the country,' he said, no longer smarting from Scotland's agonising defeat. 'Paul has all the attributes really great players have. He has two great feet, a quickness of the brain that gives him time on the ball, and he has a superb vision for passes. He is everything I like in a player and he's a good, working-class lad who just concentrates on his football.'

Ferguson believed England had not yet utilised Scholes in his best position, as the Scot moved him from a centre-forward back into the middle of the park, where he could influence play with his vision. 'It is not clear-cut what position England want to play him in,' he told the *Sun*. 'Now Keegan has come round to the view that Scholes is his main man. He is their most important player. The position we have settled him in is best, not just in behind the front two. There is nobody better at ghosting in the penalty box – he needs to be able to make those runs from deep.'

Keegan echoed the calls for Scholes to fire England to Euro glory. 'I am always looking for Paul Scholes to deliver,' he told the *Daily Mail*. 'The great asset about him is that he can play in midfield, win the ball and work hard, but that he has got tremendous ability to get on the end of things. I know he can do a number of jobs for me. Paul is adaptable and that gives you fluidity. He can make things happen in different areas. There are not many players like that, and it makes him important in that respect. Of course the icing on the cake is that he scores goals – and goals win football matches. He has scored five for me and that just proves how valuable he is.'

Scholes, meanwhile, admitted he was relishing the free role given in the middle of the park, and believed the national side needed to earn the admiration of the watching public before considering themselves legend. 'The pressure is on the strikers to score, not me,' he told the *Sun*. 'If I get one, I'm a hero but, if I don't, I won't get slagged off. If I score it is a bonus.'

The memories of the World Cup in France still played heavily on Scholes's mind, particularly a missed chance that could have put the team beyond Argentina in St Etienne. 'I should have scored and if I had that would have been 3–1 and we would have gone through,' he continued. 'But you can't change things now. When we came home to that welcome after the World Cup it was embarrassing – we had only got to the last 16. It's no good playing well and getting to the first round, we need to play well and be successful.'

Ahead of the finals England held friendlies with Brazil, Malta and Ukraine. A 1–1 draw with the former world champions served to increase the weight of expectation on Kevin Keegan's men, which was followed by a 2–0 win over the Ukraine and a 2–1 victory over the Maltese minnows. Scholes started all three games as Keegan's first-choice side began to take shape.

England were again handed a tough draw for the finals in a group that included Romania, Germany and Portugal, meaning getting through the group stages would involve victory over two much-fancied sides. England's adventures kicked off against Portugal on 12 June in Eindhoven, home of Dutch giants PSV. The Portuguese boasted a formidable side with Fernando Couto, Manuel Rui Costa and Luís Figo – whom Scholes had faced earlier in the season with Manchester United.

'Figo is the best player in the world right now,' he told the *Mirror* ahead of the showdown. 'He can beat people and create chances for himself, and also creates them for others.' England fielded a strong line-up, with a tantalising duo of youth and experience in attack as Michael Owen lined up alongside Alan Shearer. The Neville brothers provided cover as full backs while Tony Adams and Sol Campbell formed a formidable defensive partnership in the centre. David Beckham and Steve McManaman took the wide positions, while Paul Ince and Scholes marshalled the centre of the park.

Fittingly it was Scholes, given licence to roam, who got England off to a dream start, finding the net inside five minutes and, when McManaman doubled the advantage on 18 minutes, the Three Lions were on the verge of claiming an early scalp in the tournament. Portugal rallied and hit back four minutes later as Figo bagged a wonderful long-range strike to haul his side back into the contest; and, when Pinto levelled the scores seven minutes before half time, England had squandered a glorious opportunity. The game was won on the hour mark as Gomez finished a neat move to break English hearts. Scholes and Shearer both had glorious opportunities to force an equaliser, but fell agonisingly short of the mark as the match ended in defeat.

Five days later England met Germany in a titanic tussle in sleepy Belgium. The Three Lions had not beaten their old rivals in competition since the World Cup final in 1966, but luck was on their side today as an Alan Shearer header after 53 minutes proved enough to settle the match. Scholes was replaced by Nick Barmby after 72 minutes as England clung on for a famous victory.

England returned to the Stadio Communial in Charleroi knowing that a draw against Romania would be enough to see them through to the knockout stages. Their preparation for the match was severely hampered when David Seaman got injured in the warm-up, giving Nigel Martyn a rare opportunity to appear in the finals of a major tournament. Christian Chivu scored after 22 minutes as a nervy England struggled against their dogged opponents; but Alan Shearer and Michael Owen hit back shortly before half time to give England a priceless lead – and leave them 45 minutes away from a place in the next round.

The second half proved to be a nightmare for England as Munteanu restored parity within three minutes of the restart. The remainder of the second half proved a scrappy affair, with neither side looking worthy of a place in the next round; but, with a minute left to play, the match swung in favour of Romania. Scholes's United teammate Phil Neville brought down Viorel Moldovan in the area, and Ganea netted from the spot to put his side through to the quarter-finals. England had failed to make it through the group stages, as defensive lapses were punished in a roller coaster of emotions for the travelling supporters. Fan skirmishes marred much of the tournament, eventually won by France, with England fans bearing the brunt of the media backlash against football violence.

For the first time in history the World Cup would be hosted in Asia, with Korea and Japan lodging a joint bid to host the 2002 finals. England were pitted against Germany, Finland, Albania and Greece in the qualification group.

As a warm-up for the qualifiers, England met France in a friendly match in Paris. After a disastrous showing in Holland and Belgium, a good performance against the World and European champions would give the Three Lions plenty of encouragement ahead of the qualifiers, due to start in October. Coach Kevin Keegan dropped Michael Owen in favour of Andy Cole and put Scholes in as a deep-lying second striker. France were back playing in front of their home crowd and there was a party atmosphere in the Stade de France, but a tentative game finished 1–1, with Michael Owen coming off the bench to claim an 86th-minute equaliser.

With Wembley Stadium – the home of football – due to be demolished, the last game on the hallowed turf would fittingly be the home tie against Germany, the opponents when Wembley stadium witnessed its finest hour in 1966. Germany were out to spoil the farewell party and their 1–0 victory was far from the perfect ending to the historic stadium. But, despite the intensity and weight of history placed on the players, Scholes felt it was just another three points England needed to pick up in order to make the finals.

'I don't care if it's the first game at Wembley or the last match,' he is quoted in the *Sun* as saying 'That stuff doesn't mean anything to me. It's for others to talk about that – it's for England to win the game. The players must not get sucked in to what is happening around us. We know that it's just another game at Wembley. OK, it's fair to knock it down, but to us, it's a World Cup qualifier. Everyone is talking about the old days but we have to go out there and win the match,' he continued. 'That must be the only thing on our minds.'

England had tasted recent success over the Germans in their ill-fated Euro 2000 campaign, but Scholes was quick to play down any overconfidence from the Three Lions. 'All it did was show that we can beat them,' he said. 'It may give us more belief but I don't think it will have a psychological advantage. Germany were not in the best of spirits and they will be this time. It is going to be tough.'

Ahead of the game Scholes's United teammate David Beckham lavished praise on Scholes, underlining his importance to the national side ahead of the forthcoming qualification campaign. 'Paul gets forward, scores goals, and for a little lad – just look at the size of him – the way he gets up and heads the ball and the goals he scores with his head is something not a lot of players can do', he said. 'As long as he's in the team, he'll always have a chance of scoring and producing things like that. I'm sure Paul's happy with the way he's playing, – the goals he's getting and the way he's performing for United and England. He's doing very well.'

Having cemented his place in the heart of England's midfield, Scholes was perfectly placed to influence what was a huge spectacle. But it was his foul 30 yards from goal that gave Germany a site at goal. Dietmar Hamann struck a skidding free kick the beat David Seaman to nestle in the bottom corner. The result left the Wembley faithful dumbstruck in the pouring October rain – and Kevin Keegan announced his decision to quit as national coach, believing he was not up to the job.

Howard Wilkinson again took temporary charge of the national side in the wake of Keegan's departure, with England facing a tricky match away to Finland just four days after the agonising defeat to Germany. They dominated the game, but were made to settle for a goalless draw, with Ray Parlour unlucky not to grab all three points, as he could only hit the crossbar late on. Former under-21 coach Peter Taylor took charge of the national side for the next game, a friendly against Italy in November, but the Azzurri claimed a 1–0 victory thanks to Rino Gattuso's second-half effort. Scholes missed the match, with United teammate Nicky Butt staking his claim for a central midfield berth.

Talk began to emerge that a foreigner might take charge of the English national side, an unprecedented move that drew many critics. The Football Association, however, were not to be deterred and announced the appointment of Swedish tactician Sven-Göran Eriksson in early 2001. Eriksson had won plenty of admirers in charge of Roman club Lazio and made history as the first foreigner to lead England.

Despite seeming unconcerned by matters other than football regarding the national side, Scholes spoke out against the appointment of Eriksson. 'It's the England team and I would like to see them with an English manager,' he told the Associated Press. 'I don't know why they didn't give Peter Taylor the full-time job instead of asking him to take care of things for a while, especially as he is English. Peter seems a really nice bloke and a good manager.'

It was a rare outburst from Scholes, voicing his backing for Peter Taylor in the knowledge that Eriksson would soon know how he felt. The Swede's first game in charge was a friendly at home to Spain, who, like England, struggled in major tournaments despite a wealth of footballing talent. While many held grave reservations, a resounding 3–0 victory silenced the critics as goals from Nick Barmby, Emile Heskey and Ugo Ehiogu sealed the win. Scholes was afforded a starting place for the game, but was withdrawn for Ehiogu shortly after half time as Eriksson rang the changes. It was to be a feature of his England tenure, particularly in friendlies, to impose numerous substitutions to get a good look at the best England had to offer.

Qualification resumed in March as Anfield played host to the return fixture with Sweden. Despite his criticism of Eriksson's appointment, Scholes confessed he was won over by the Swede once training was under way. 'I've been impressed with things under Sven even though I wasn't with the team for a long time against Spain,' he said. 'I was only with the squad for two days so I'll get to know more in the coming weeks. We desperately need six points to lift us off the bottom of the table.'

England were still searching for their first win in the group stages and Scholes admitted the squad could take nothing for granted against the Finns. 'We have to win these games just to bring us back into contention and then hopefully we will go to Germany and get some points there,' he told the *Daily Record*. 'Finland will be trying like mad, so it will be more difficult. Finland are a good side,' he continued. 'A few of their players play in Europe and the Premiership so it will be difficult.'

Michael Owen and David Beckham scored in each half to settle England's nerves, but a Gary Neville own goal set up a tense finish. The match finished 2–1 and England had their first victory of the qualification campaign.

England travelled to Albania confident of victory over their unfancied hosts, but it took 75 minutes to prise open the dogged Albanian rearguard. It was Michael Owen who finally broke the deadlock, latching on to a Scholes through ball to fire underneath the goalkeeper. Scholes promptly doubled England's advantage with five minutes remaining after neat work from

United teammate Andy Cole, who fired in the third in the closing minutes after Altin Rraklli had reduced the deficit.

England continued their great start under Eriksson with a 4–0 victory over Mexico at Derby County's Pride Park Stadium in May. Scholes opened the scoring inside five minutes – with Robbie Fowler, David Beckham and Teddy Sheringham adding the others. A dominant performance over the South Americans would do little to worry Greece in England's next qualifier, according to Scholes. 'I don't think that will have scared Greece,' he told the *Scotsman*. 'They are a very good team but it was nice to get that early goal, it gives a lot of confidence.'

England travelled to Athens knowing a win would put them back in contention in the group, and Eriksson kept faith with the side that had so convincingly brushed past Mexico 12 days earlier – with the only change being David Seaman's return in goal. Scholes made it three goals in his last three games with the opener on 64 minutes, while David Beckham made the result safe in the dying moments.

England looked strong under Eriksson and indeed rejuvenated by fresh ideas, but the unbeaten run soon came to an end in a friendly with Holland at White Hart Lane. Again Scholes was afforded only 45 minutes as Eriksson tinkered with his side, utilising the strength of England's squad. First-half goals from Mark van Bommel and Ruud van Nistelrooy proved too much for England, who lost all shape under the constant changes in personnel.

Perhaps the defining moment of Eriksson's reign – and one of England's greatest ever performances – came in their World Cup qualifier with Germany on 1 September 2001. England's pride had been severely wounded as Germany gatecrashed the Wembley leaving party almost a year earlier. Revenge would be sweet for the Three Lions, who tore their opponents apart in Munich's Olympic Stadium. Scholes lined up in his customary central midfield role alongside Liverpool's Steven Gerrard, who had begun to establish himself as a first-team regular for Eriksson. The young Liverpudlian won the plaudits from Scholes. 'Stevie is very similar to Roy Keane, and Vieira as well,' he told the *Birmingham Post*. 'I think he has got everything. He can pass, score goals and make goals as well.'

Of his new, blossoming midfield partnership, he said, 'It has worked well up to now. We both like to go forward and understand that we need to look out and work for each other. It's partly down to communication but mostly it's instinct. That gives me more confidence to get into goal-scoring positions as I know that, if I go forward, there will always be someone there who can fill in for me.'

Scholes has admitted that the weight of expectation playing for your country can exceed that of club level, particularly in highly charged derby games against the likes of Germany. 'You feel the expectation with England a bit more,' he said. 'A lot is made of how different international football is from the Premiership, but you have just got to do the things that got you into the squad in the first place. With Manchester United, you don't seem to feel the pressure, but it's more with England,' he confessed. 'It's massive, it's nationwide, it's the whole country and everyone is writing about England.'

Any pressure would have been increased as Germany pulled ahead in the sixth minute through Carsten Jancker, who poked home past the onrushing David Seaman – much to the delight of the Bavarian crowd. England rallied, and drew level seven minutes later, thanks to a composed finish from Michael Owen. Buoyed by the goal, England began to get a grip on the match and were rewarded on the strike of half time, with Gerrard hitting a glorious low drive past the despairing dive of Oliver Kahn.

The second half began as the first had ended, with England hitting the back of the net. Michael Owen bagged his second with a near-post finish that surprised Kahn. Owen became the first England player since Scholes to score a hat-trick for the national side when he produced another impeccable finish into the top right-hand corner on 66 minutes; and, when Emile Heskey slotted home on 74, England had landed a devastating blow on their old enemy.

Any doubts over Eriksson's appointment were quickly forgotten in the wake of this remarkable victory on German soil and England fans began to gaze hopefully to the east with hope of a trip to the World Cup. However, the three points picked up at the expense of Germany would mean little if England failed to beat Albania four days later as Newcastle's St James's Park stadium played host to the national side. England started strongly, buoyed by the fanatical Geordie following, and Scholes could have broken the deadlock inside four minutes, but he blazed over a speculative 25-yard drive.

England were becoming increasingly reliant on Michael Owen as a source of goals and the young Liverpool star delivered once again to break the deadlock after being fed by a measured pass from Scholes. In the wake of Alan Shearer's international retirement, Scholes soon had a mobile, pacey striker who could latch onto his now trademark raking pass. However, any hopes of another cricket score were quelled by a gritty and resilient Albania, who withstood any further damage until the 88th minute, when substitute Robbie Fowler ran through on goal to delicately chip the keeper and settle the tie.

England had now moved to the top of qualifying Group 9 – ahead of Germany, thanks to their superior goal difference – knowing that victory over Greece at Old Trafford would secure a place in the 2002 World Cup finals in Korea and Japan.

Throughout the qualifying campaign Scholes had proved a permanent fixture in the side as the midfield enforcer who could bring others into the game with his range of passing; but the spectre of the sending-off against Sweden years earlier still played on his mind. His teammates, however, believed his battling qualities were reminiscent of former Manchester United great Bryan Robson, who dominated the Old Trafford midfield ruthlessly.

'He scores like goals like Bryan Robson did for England,' Phil Neville told the *Mirror*. 'He can have a quiet game, but then comes up with a goal. He ghosts into the box unmarked and, before the opposition knows what has hit them, he has found the back of the net.'

Scholes confessed his delight at being compared to one of Manchester United's most dynamic captains. He said, 'Bryan Robson was a hero of mine and I think I've tried to take into my game the way he went forward and scored goals. He was a better player than me,' Scholes continued, careful to ensure his modesty shone through. 'He tackled and defended a lot more and had more presence on the pitch. But I like to get forward the way he did.'

Having found the back of the net in Athens when England travelled to Greece in the first meeting between the two sides, Scholes would have fancied his chances of firing his country to the Far East, with only himself and David Beckham starting every match under Eriksson, but the stubborn Greeks had no intention of laying down their arms at Old Trafford. With Greece holding a slender 2–1 advantage as injury time approached, and with automatic qualification hopes lying in tatters, David Beckham stepped up with one of his most memorable moments in an England shirt. The outcast of the previous World Cup, the petulant boy who had left England's quest in ruins, stepped up to fire an inch-perfect free kick past Antonios Nikopolidis and send England through to the finals.

Yet again, England's qualification campaign had been fraught with difficulties, a seesaw of emotion and elation, but a ticket to Japan and Korea had been booked, and Sven-Göran Eriksson's England could plan their assault on the first World Cup to be held in Asia. Despite the elation of making the finals, Scholes chose to be critical of his own performance, admitting he could have done more to put the game to bed before Beckham's last-minute magic.

'I was terrible,' he told the *Mail on Sunday*. 'You have got to be honest with yourself at all times. I have played 39 matches for England and a lot of people have suggested I haven't had a poor game before the Greece match. But I don't know about that, my performance against Germany last year wasn't too clever either. Looking back on last Saturday, though, it was just terrible, definitely the worst I have played in an England shirt.

'This time a few others struggled as well,' he continued. 'Still, I am not going to have a go at anybody else because that is not right. I believe that when this sort of thing happens I can look no further than myself and what I did.'

Scholes, despite being a permanent fixture in the side, rejected rumours that Eriksson had written his name on the team sheet first. 'Not after Greece he won't,' Scholes admitted. 'When we got back into the dressing room every player was naturally elated about making the finals. We simply couldn't believe the way we had played to get there. It was, to be honest, a disheartening way to do it,' he said, in a typically blunt insight into his meticulous character. 'I read that 78 per cent of my passes went to teammates, so it could have been worse. Still, it could have been better than that. I just started badly and got worse.'

Scholes's performances had drawn praise from all the four corners of the globe, which were about to be united in football's largest ever party. Dutch defender Frank de Boer hailed Scholes as the finest English talent, and the man to fire them to glory.

'The English player I admire most is Scholes,' he told the *Daily Mail*. 'He is the most complete player I have seen in a long time and reminds me of Johan Cruyff. He always seems to be in the right place at the right time and scores important goals at crucial times. What impresses me most is his versatility. Sometimes it is a detraction to call a player versatile, but this is a compliment. He scores with his head but he is not tall, he scores tap ins but he can shoot from range.

'He is physically tough, though not big or strong by comparison to his opponents. Scholes has been in the England setup for four years and has easily been the team's most consistent performer. His international goals-per-game ratio is phenomenal and he is also a playmaker of quality. Perhaps he is not the team's most high profile player, but he is the heartbeat.'

The arrival of Juan Verón at Manchester United had forced Scholes into the second striker's role, one he had not adopted since his youth, but Eriksson was happy to utilise Scholes in his preferred central midfield slot for the time being. 'I think Paul can play in central midfield, as a second striker, at outside right or outside left,' said the Swede. 'He is not a defender, but in all other places he is excellent. With England, however, he has always played in central midfield and I see no reason why I should change that.'

Scholes had the opportunity for redemption in November when England hosted Sweden in an intriguing tie that pitted Eriksson against his home country. In truth, the match proved to be a scrappy, disjointed affair with both teams limping to a 1–1 draw. Scholes continued his starting run under Eriksson in a team bereft of scoring sensation Michael Owen, with Kevin Phillips a surprise choice to start despite some devastating performances at club level. Trevor Sinclair won England a soft penalty on the half-hour mark, which Beckham promptly dispatched, but the visitors equalised shortly before half time to ensure the spoils were shared.

England duties were put on hold until the New Year, when the Three Lions travelled to Holland for a tricky friendly at the Amsterdam Arena, home of Dutch giants Ajax. Eriksson continued his policy of testing all the English talent at his disposal, with Bolton forward Michael Ricketts starting the match alongside Darius Vassell in a makeshift England attack. Dutch poacher Patrick Kluivert put the home side ahead on 26 minutes with a typically clinical finish, but the day would belong to debutant Vassell, who scored a terrific acrobatic volley to save his country from defeat. Scholes was afforded a starting berth but was replaced by Joe Cole with a little less than a quarter of an hour remaining.

England continued a succession of challenging friendlies with the visit of Italy to Leeds's Elland Road stadium. The Azzurri would see any victory on English soil as scant consolation for defeat in Rome in qualifying for the 1998 World Cup, and they were to be rewarded for a bullish away performance with a 2–1 win. Eriksson had wanted to field a full-strength side with the finals now in sight, but injuries to Scholes and other key men ensured the match became a further showcase of England's strength in depth – rather than first-choice 11.

Scholes was restored to the starting line-up for England's final warm-up game against Paraguay on 17 April in a match hosted at Liverpool's Anfield. Scholes was given the first half to prove his worth to the England manager, but England proved sluggish. Having found the net through Owen on four minutes, England took their foot off the accelerator and failed to breach the South Americans during the remainder of the first half. For perhaps the first time Eriksson's halftime tinkering paid off as England started the half fresh and rejuvenated, finding the net through Danny Murphy shortly after the restart. Darius Vassell showed his debut goal was no fluke by netting a third, and Roberto Ayala put through his own net to secure a 4–0 win as the English fans bid their team farewell ahead of the World Cup finals.

III

Sven-Göran Eriksson had won over the supporters and pundits alike as England powered to the finals, and the Swede admitted that, with players like Paul Scholes in the team, the fans could start dreaming of World Cup glory.

'I think we have extremely good players such as David Beckham, Michael Owen, Steven Gerrard and Paul Scholes,' he told the Associated Press. 'There are many others but, if I said those four players are world-class, then it is not a surprise. Hopefully people around the world will say more names after the World Cup. Football is about many things but one thing is not to be afraid, no matter how important your opponent is. Why should we have the idea to lose against any team in the world?'

Changes in the rules sparked interest and controversy ahead of the tournament, with the World Cup always providing a dubious spectacle for international players diving and cheating to gain an advantage, with referees promising to be more stringent. Scholes, meanwhile, said simulation would always be a factor in football if it gets your team an advantage. 'To be honest, I know nothing about the latest so-called clampdown,' he told London's *Evening Standard*. 'If it means trying to get a penalty for your team, I am sure players will do it. If you go to win a penalty and you get the slightest touch, you go down. It's up to the referee then, with what he interprets as a dive. Personally I can't see referees giving out too many cards for diving. I don't think players will have to adapt too much to the ways referees will handle World Cup games. Referees will make good and bad decisions, so I am not too worried about them.'

With his position at Manchester United undermined by the arrival of Juan Verón, Scholes admitted he found it a relief to come back to the England setup, where he could ply his trade in the more favoured central midfield position. However, he did fear for his England place after a disappointing campaign at Old Trafford.

'I met up with England and I was back playing where I was used to,' he told the *Sunday Mirror*. 'The England manager never said anything to me, there was never a problem because I didn't raise it. I just tried hard not to think about it, but it was preying on my mind.'

Scholes confessed England's safe passage to the knockout stages was less than secure with a tricky group ahead of them. 'It will be tough to get out of this group with Argentina, Sweden and Nigeria, who are three extremely good teams, but I like to think I can take the pressure in a big match,' he said. 'As a footballer you want to play in the big games, and to play in the big games you have got to handle the pressure. Personally, I think we all have something to prove. When you haven't done much in a major tournament for 36 years you have to go a long way to prove you are up there with the best.'

Acclimatising to the harsh, humid conditions in Asia would take some getting used to, and England had to negotiate friendly matches against Portugal and co-hosts South Korea before the group stages got under way. The stadium shook under a sea of red each time South Korea played. Eriksson adopted a new 4–3–3 formation and it appeared to pay dividends, as Scholes crossed for Owen to put England ahead after 26 minutes. But South Korea were well marshalled by Dutch tactician Guus Hiddink and would prove a difficult prospect for many of the more fancied European sides on their own soil; and Park Ji-Sung equalised on 52 minutes as the match finished an almost predictable 1–1.

England's World Cup warm-up concluded with another draw, this time two goals apiece with African powerhouses Cameroon. Samuel Eto'o fired the Africans ahead within five minutes, but a beautifully crafted pass from Scholes set up Vassell to net within ten minutes. Geremi restored Cameroon's lead just before the hour but Robbie Fowler rescued a point for the Three Lions in stoppage time. England escaped without any injuries and were ready to start the group stages, full of confidence for a good showing in the Far East.

Eriksson's side were pitted against Nigeria (who had won many fans with their carnival football at the previous World Cup), Sweden (another interesting tie that brought home the absurdity of having a foreign manager) and Argentina (another old enemy). First up were Sweden in sun-drenched Saitama on 2 June.

England were full of hope with Beckham overcoming the dreaded metatarsal injury. And, with the celebration of the Queen's Jubilee, the flag of Saint George had never flown higher, especially after Sol Campbell headed home a collector's-item international goal after 26 minutes to send the visiting fans wild.

The most pivotal match in the group stages was the Sapporo tussle between England and Argentina. Scholes was still smarting from the 1998 defeat in St Etienne and hoped to gain revenge in the Far East.

'Argentina are fancied by many to win it but I don't see why we can't compete with them,' he told the *Sun*. 'The key to success in big games is handling the pressure properly. You have to treat it like any other match and we shot that last year in Munich when we beat Germany 5–1. We proved then that we can be a big nation.'

Scholes confessed that, despite his personal achievements in an England shirt, and a series of swashbuckling displays, he could not consider himself an England great until he achieved international success.

'I still have to prove myself,' he continued. 'I have never got past the last 16 and to be regarded as world class you have to go a lot further.'

Wounds inflicted by the South Americans in both 1986 and 1998 had failed to heal, but England were able to exact a small manner of revenge with a 1–0 victory. Fittingly, the goal came from the right boot of David Beckham, who had rebuilt his golden boy reputation after it had been shattered four years earlier against Argentina. The game was a high-octane affair, with Scholes busy in central midfield contending with the mercurial Juan Verón and the terrier Diego Simeone. On the stroke of half time, England were awarded a lifeline when Michael Owen was felled by Pochettino in the box. The tension built to a crescendo before Beckham lashed the penalty hard, low and straight through Cavellero in the Argentine goal.

England were under the cosh for much of the second half, with Pablo Aimar living up to his billing as one of the hottest young prospects at the tournament. However, England were not to be denied and claimed a sweet victory over their rivals. Scholes produced a mammoth display to dwarf United teammate Verón in the centre of the park, and the England midfielder considers that it was one of the best victories of his career.

'This feels ten times better than Munich,' he told the *Sun*. 'I can't describe how good this feels. Munich was great at the time – but this is the World Cup finals and Argentina. Who knows what message this will send out to the rest of the world? But Argentina are one of the favourites and we have not only beaten them – but beaten them well. I am sure other teams will stand up and take notice of England after this. We have still got a tough game against Nigeria to take care of but this puts us in a great position.'

And Scholes was delighted for teammate David Beckham, who finally put the pain of St Etienne behind him. 'After what happened to Becks four years ago against Argentina it was great for him to get the winning goal,' Scholes continued. 'It is so nice to get one back over them. I didn't envy him taking the penalty but that is his job and, thankfully for us, he smashed it in.'

The plaudits did not stop there, as Scholes lavished praise on fellow midfield enforcer Nicky Butt. 'He was magnificent. He hadn't played for five weeks, so to turn in that level of performance was marvellous.'

England's task of qualifying for the knockout stages had been aided greatly by victory over Argentina, but they needed to avoid defeat against Nigeria to be assured of a place in the next round. Scholes spearheaded the England midfield along with United teammate Nicky Butt, who won praise from across the footballing community for his displays in the Far East, including Brazilian legend Pele. Scholes had a trademark 25-yard drive fall agonisingly wide on the stroke of half time. England huffed and puffed in the strangling heat, but were unable to break down the powerful Africans, resulting in a goalless draw, which proved enough to see the Three Lions through after Sweden had held Argentina to a 1–1 draw to top the group.

England faced another Scandinavian nation in Niigata for a place in the quarter-finals, with Denmark providing the opposition for Eriksson's men. The match proved comfortable for England, who took their chances clinically as they eased to a 3–0 victory. Scholes was replaced by Kieran Dyer shortly after half time with Eriksson aware that a place in the next round was all but assured. England had taken the lead through a freak own goal inside five minutes, with Michael Owen and Emile Heskey both netting before half time to secure a scoreline that perhaps flattered England. But no matter: a quarter-final against the stars of Brazil awaited.

Shizuoka played host to the most eagerly anticipated of the

quarter-finals as England, workmanlike and dogged, faced Brazil, who had flair and ruthlessness in equal measure. Scholes told the Associated Press England fancied their chances of victory against the much-lauded South Americans, buoyed by their win over Argentina in the group stages.

'There's no point of going into games thinking you can't win. We proved that against Argentina,' he said. 'Brazil have been brilliant so far but we're getting better all the time. Now we are through to the quarter-finals. You don't get to that stage of the World Cup unless you're a half-decent team – hopefully we can go further. We know that there are big expectations back home but being over here we are a little bit away from it. I know it's a cliché, but we are taking each game as it comes and we will try to win them.'

While Eriksson had his detractors for his expressionless stance on the touchline, Scholes believes his calm approach instilled confidence in the team, particularly ahead of the game against Brazil. 'Brazil are a world-class team but we have got the players who can do well against them,' he told the *Mirror*. 'The players believe we have a very good chance. The manager is great: he puts a lot of belief in us and believes we will beat any team. We are starting to believe him now. If you make a mistake he tells us to forget about it and encourage each other. He is not a ranter and raver and he has been great for England.

'It comes from the Argentina game, beating them and playing so well when they were the favourites for the tournament. Of course it was great to beat Germany 5–1 in Munich but they had been on the slide for a bit and were maybe not as good as they had been.'

The carnival atmosphere that sweeps through the air every time the Brazilian national team play was not lost on their opponents, according to Scholes. 'The excitement of Brazil comes through to us as well,' he said. 'They are a massive team, with their history and the players they have. It's exciting when you see them play. They must have six or seven world-class players who can turn a game just like that.

'Rivaldo and Ronaldo are world stars and loom large, but we have to go out and compete with them. This could be our only chance to play them in a World Cup. These are the teams you want to play against to prove you are a good side. They don't really seem to play in set positions. At the back especially, some of them go where they want. They give you a chance and we have got the players to exploit that as well.'

With the weight of expectation from both sets of fans weighing heavily on the players, the match proved a drab affair. Michael Owen pounced to give England the lead on 23 minutes, placing the ball past the onrushing Marcos as the travelling England support began to dream of a famous victory. Brazil equalised shortly before half time after a move of devastating fluency between Ronaldinho and Rivaldo, which saw the latter poke home. Brazil's equaliser would go on to haunt Arsenal veteran David Seaman for the rest of his career.

Scholes committed a foul 40 yards from goal, which everyone expected Ronaldinho to send in to the giant Brazilian defenders Lúcio and Roque Junior. However, the Brazilian magician had other ideas, sending the ball over Seaman in a cross-cum-shot that would leave pundits guessing for days.

Despite gaining a man advantage when Ronaldinho was dismissed for a challenge on Danny Mills, England looked devoid of ideas and were forced to endure another high-octane exit in the finals of a major tournament.

So, with tournament heartbreak once again sweeping over the nation following another early exit for the national team, England duties were put on hold until September, at the start of the 2002–03 season. England faced Euro 2004 hosts Portugal in a friendly at Villa Park, but Manchester United ruled the midfielder out through injury. When Scholes started for Manchester United against Middlesbrough the following weekend, it sparked a club-versus-country row between Ferguson and Eriksson. Scholes had begun to get to grips with the supporting-striker role at Manchester United, which, with a plethora of good English midfielders to choose from, gave Eriksson another option in the national side. Scholes told the *Daily Mail*, 'I am enjoying playing up front a lot more this season. Last season I struggled and I worried it might affect my international chances.'

Sven-Göran Eriksson's England were drawn alongside Turkey, Liechtenstein, Macedonia and Slovakia in the qualification for Euro 2004 in less than two years' time. England opened their campaign with a trip to Slovakia at the Stadion SK Slovan on 12 October. The Three Lions struggled in woeful conditions against a team sensing a qualification giant-killing. Their hopes took a giant leap as they took the lead on 24 minutes through Szilard Nemeth, capitalising on some hesitant defending that sparked a heated postmortem from the England defence. Scholes had been shifted out to the left side of England's midfield, as Eriksson had struggled to find a permanent incumbent for the position. Once again, Scholes was to be punished for his versatility, playing out of position to cover for England's deficiencies.

England worked hard on an awful playing field, hoping to force an equaliser, which came from the boot of David Beckham just after the hour mark. The England captain curled in a free kick that bamboozled the Slovakian defence, dropping into the net untouched. The Three Lions had the scent of victory but found themselves thwarted at every turn until the match was inside the final ten minutes, when Michael Owen netted to give England a nervous, but gratefully received, three points. The uncertain form continued four days later with a tragic 2–2 draw at home to Macedonia at Southampton's St Mary's Stadium, England's display epitomised by David Seaman, who let a corner fly over his head and into the back of the net to condemn Eriksson's side to a home draw.

International duties were put on hold until the New Year when England hosted Australia in a friendly many expected to prove an England walkover. The exact opposite was true, however, as Australia took the match 3–1. The only thing worth remembering from an England perspective was Wayne Rooney's international bow, giving Scholes his first look at the man who would soon empty the Old Trafford coffers in a transfer from Everton.

Qualification, meanwhile, resumed in March with a trip to Liechtenstein, which England won 2–0 in an uninspiring contest in Vaduz, which set them up for the visit of Turkey four days later. The Turks were considered England's biggest threat to the top spot in the group, but another 2–0 win at the Stadium of Light saw England take an early advantage. Nervous 2–1 wins over Slovakia and Macedonia followed, with Scholes continually frustrated playing out of position. A 2–0 victory over part-timers Liechtenstein on home soil took England into the final group game on 11 October, knowing they had to avoid defeat to book their place in the finals.

Ahead of the crucial qualifier in Turkey, Scholes said England players were close to going on strike after being angered by the treatment of Rio Ferdinand, who was given an eight-month suspension for missing a drugs test, and the Manchester United midfielder admits that only the threat of expulsion from the European Championships prevented them. 'The threat not to play in this game was real, we really thought about it,' he told *FourFourTwo* magazine. 'Rio was treated badly, and we still think that now. Whether we would have gone through with the boycott, I don't really know. The threat of being chucked out of Euro 2004 was the main factor in pulling out. The papers got a bit carried away with it,' he continued. 'We were just sticking up for one of our teammates. I am sure people do that in their workplace all the time. We thought Rio was being treated unfairly, so we supported him.'

Tensions boiled over in Sukru Saracoglu Stadium, a cauldron of aggression and heat, culminating in a half-time brawl that marred what was otherwise a thoroughly professional England performance. The goalless draw was enough to put England through to the finals.

Since he had played in the unfamiliar left-sided position, the goals had dried up for Scholes, who had not scored in an England shirt since 6 June 2001. Now, going into the summer of 2004, he confessed his place in the side was in danger. 'It's gone past that actually,' he told the *Observer*. 'It definitely has been preying on my mind, but now I am trying not to think about it too much, so I don't get too anxious. I don't think I need to do anything differently. I just need my luck to change. Hopefully, if I keep on getting picked in the team, I'll get the chance to score.'

Scholes's biggest threat to his place came from Chelsea midfielder Frank Lampard, whose free-scoring antics in west London had found him knocking on the door for an international start, and Scholes admits that he could not begrudge the former West Ham star a place in the side. 'I'm in the team to score goals and, if I'm not doing that, I know there's a chance I won't be picked,' he said. 'I know I'm not expected to get as many as the strikers, but I am expected to score. If that's not happening, I'm not contributing as much as I should be to the team.

'It's not just about me, either. When there are players like Frank Lampard having a great season, they probably don't deserve to be given a place in the starting line-up. If the manager were to pick him instead of me, I would wish him all the best because I know I've not done what I should have been doing for England. Frank is playing well and I've had a good run in the team without scoring any goals. I still love playing for England and I think we have a really good chance in Euro 2004 now that everyone's fit. We all want to do as well as we can and go as far as we can, but from my own point of view I know I had better start scoring.'

Meanwhile, Bobby Charlton, hero for both England and Manchester United, said Eriksson must keep faith in Scholes if he was to stand any chance of glory in Portugal. 'Paul loves the game and scoring goals', he told the *Express*. 'He has instant control, vision and awareness. He is a great player. If Paul Scholes, the Nevilles and Nicky Butt are playing for England, you want them to do well.'

Charlton also responded to the club-versus-country row, particularly in the wake of Rio Ferdinand's eight-month ban for missing a drugs test. 'We should be doing better in these championships but our game has got so big it is very hard to keep players fresh', he continued. 'The fact that Rio Ferdinand is not going is a big blow because you have got to have your best players if you are going to win these tournaments and Rio is our best defender. So I am not thinking that we are going to win it. I would much rather think that than be overconfident.'

The European Championship finals pitted England in another tough group, with holders France, dogged Croatia and unfancied Switzerland forming the competition. The game against France drew all the pre-tournament attention and French legend Zinédine Zidane confessed his side would be very wary of the English threat.

'We will be absolutely at the top of our game immediately', he told the *News of the World*. 'It is good to start with a big match – and it is crucial to do well in the first game of a major tournament. England, for me, are a team that cannot be disregarded as contenders for the title and I mean that sincerely. Victory over them would give us a massive psychological boost.

Gerrard is a young player on the way to greatness. Owen is a great player and Scholes is dangerous as well,' he said.

Meanwhile Scholes's United and England teammate Gary Neville chose to draw comparisons between Zidane and the red-headed midfielder. 'He can control the ball, he can hold up the play or keep the ball moving – similar to the things Zidane gives the French,' he told the *Daily Mail*. 'I think he is a different class. One of the best I have ever played with. It doesn't really matter if he has players all round him, he can still see a pass. People go on about the goalscoring but a player like that doesn't need to score goals to justify his place in the team. Some of his passing and moving is incredible.'

Arsenal's French contingent seemed keen to start a war of words despite the compliments flying back and forth before the finals. 'I read last week that Robert Pirès thinks they're going to beat us 3-1,' Scholes told *The Times*. 'They are just ultra-confident. That's the way they feel, it is maybe just the way they are. It is a motivation, but it would be nice to say that after the game, to say that it wound us up. A few of their players have had a lot to say about our defence. At the end of the day, all that matters is what is happening out on the pitch.'

Meanwhile, Scholes gave the earliest indication that he could curtail his international career. 'This might be my last tournament,' he continued. 'I hope it won't be, but the way I am playing at the moment, there is every chance. People have said to me before that I am not someone who relies on confidence, but I do,' he confessed. 'I never thought my goalless streak would go on so long and it is worrying. It happened at United a couple of years ago, when I didn't score my first goal until November. It does affect you.'

Scholes reckoned the Arsenal players could be arrogant with their success, but on the pitch he had the utmost respect for them. 'It is always nice to test yourself against the best,' he told the *Independent*. 'There is no doubt [Patrick Vieira] is going to be one of the best holding players in the tournament. When I play against him I try to keep away from him, keep the ball away from him because his legs are so long. You put all the French team together and you see how much strength they have, but we do believe we can beat them.'

Scholes continued to praise Eriksson for his continued support through the goal drought, saying, 'He has always spoken up for me, and has never left me out. That's always important to a player when he's feeling a bit of pressure and I just hope I can pay him back. I was very frustrated when I didn't score. The good thing is that I still have the confidence to make those runs into the box. I still believe in myself enough to do that and, despite what I've read in the papers, I'm happy to play out on the left. I have the freedom to roam about a bit with the guarantee of having two in the middle.'

The match took place in the imposing Estadio da Luz, home of Sporting Lisbon. Scholes started on the left with Steven Gerrard and Frank Lampard taking the central midfield berths, while David Beckham occupied his captain's role on the right. Lampard justified his place in the midfield by opening the scoring on thirty minutes after connecting with a David Beckham delivery. And the England skipper had the chance to put the game beyond

France in the second half after Wayne Rooney was felled by Mikael Silvestre in the area. Incredibly, Beckham failed the resulting spot kick, as Barthez made a fine save. England's failure to increase their lead came back to haunt them in injury time, as Zinédine Zidane proved far more ruthless, curling in a glorious free kick before netting from the penalty spot after Gerrard's uncharacteristic mistake.

Despite all the talk, Scholes endured another barren game in front of goal against France, but Eriksson sprang to his defence once again, claiming he was never a concern. 'Paul Scholes – you can't be worried about Paul Scholes,' he told the Associated Press.

Despite fellow professionals and past masters singing his praises, the lack of goals from someone so often associated with hitting the back of the net made Scholes a media scapegoat. However, goals were not going to be a problem for the Three Lions in their next group game against Switzerland in Coimbra, as England got their campaign back on track with a comfortable victory.

Wayne Rooney netted a double each side of half time to become the youngest ever scorer in the European Championships, a record that would soon be broken by Swiss youngster Johan Vonlanthen. The Everton youngster opened the scoring after 23 minutes after heading home Michael Owen's measured cross. Substitute Darius Vassell proved his increasing worth as an impact substitute by setting up the Liverpudlian to bag his second, before Steven Gerrard made the result safe with less than ten minutes to go.

Scholes was replaced by Owen Hargreaves after 70 minutes

with the Swiss offering little to trouble the dominant England midfield. With Gerrard and Lampard becoming Eriksson's preferred options in the middle of the park, Scholes increasingly found himself isolated on the left, relying on Arsenal full-back Ashley Cole to provide extra width down the flanks. The result left England needing only a draw in their final group game with Croatia to secure a place in the quarter-finals, but Eriksson's side swept to a morale-boosting 4–2 victory in a match that saw Scholes finally break his international hoodoo.

The game got off to a nightmare start as Croatia took a sixth-minute lead through Niko Kovac, who pounced on some hesitant England defending. They held onto their lead until five minutes before the interval, when Scholes intervened with a crucial goal. Scholes had managed to break free from the shackles of the left midfield position and arrived with a typically perfect run into the area to head home a priceless equaliser. Buoyed by the goal, England took the lead on the interval after neat interplay between Scholes and Michael Owen, who exchanged passes to put Wayne Rooney through on goal – the youngster made no mistake and sent England into half time a goal to the good.

Rooney grabbed his second on 68 minutes, only to be pegged back by Igor Tudor's 75th-minute effort; but the breathless encounter was settled by Frank Lampard with ten minutes remaining as England powered through to the quarter-finals.

Eriksson's men were pitted against hosts Portugal in an ill-tempered quarter-final back in the Estadio da Luz in Lisbon. Eriksson kept faith with the players who had put England through to this stage and the move paid dividends as they took the lead on three minutes through Michael Owen, who placed a delicate shot over Ricardo to stun the home crowd. England had 87 minutes to cling on and claim a priceless victory, but a 37th-minute injury to *wunderkind* Wayne Rooney sparked the beginning of England's downfall. With the weight of expectation on the teenager's shoulders, a broken metatarsal would spell the end of his campaign prematurely.

Darius Vassell, so often utilised late in the game when his pace could trouble weary legs, was now put into battle. England held off the Portuguese onslaught until the 83rd minute, when Tottenham Hotspur youngster Hélder Postiga netted the equaliser to send the tie into extra time. Scholes, too, had to be replaced by Phil Neville on 57 minutes, as his talent was being wasted on the left side of midfield. Scholes left the field for the last time as an England player.

Portugal legend Manuel Rui Costa edged the hosts ahead, pouncing on an error from Scholes's replacement, Neville. However, the trial 'silver-goal' ruling could not save Portugal, as Frank Lampard struck after 115 minutes to send the tie to penalties. Scholes and England had suffered penalty heartbreak before and that night in the Portuguese capital proved to be no different. After Darius Vassell missed from the spot, goalkeeper Ricardo placed the ball past David James to send the hosts through, to the joy of the partisan crowd in the capital.

So Scholes saw his last international action on 24 June 2004, with the Three Lions crashing out of another major tournament in a match filled with drama, disappointment and incident. That August Scholes revealed his decision to quit international football at the age of 29, to prolong his career with Manchester United and limit trips away from his young family.

'I've been considering quitting international football for some time now,' he told Manchester United's official website. 'I started my England career in 1997 and have enjoyed seven years of great football, playing in the best competitions, with some of the best players, under the best managers. I would like to thank everyone at England for the wonderful years I had playing for the team and all the experience I gained. I wish them all the best and good luck for the future. Euro 2004 was fantastic but afterwards I felt the time was right for myself and my family to make it my last England appearance.'

Meanwhile, coach Sven-Göran Eriksson reluctantly accepted Scholes's decision, as he told the Football Association's official website. 'Paul and I have been talking about this since Euro 2004 and, while he remained a key part of my plans for the England team, I fully respect his decision. He has a very special talent and it has been a pleasure working so closely with him.'

Scholes admits that, in the following months, the Swede did attempt to lure him out of his international slumber. However, he maintained he would resist any offers from the former Lazio coach: 'Sven has spoken to me and said the door is open,' he told the *Sunday Mirror*. 'I appreciate his call but I don't think I will walk through that door. Changing my mind hasn't entered my head. There are a lot of reasons why I took the decision.'

With Manchester United spending big in the transfer market to compete with the emerging threat of Arsenal and Chelsea, Scholes acknowledged that he needed to concentrate on events at Old

Trafford as a priority. 'I need to be at the top of my game', he continued. 'The way we are playing at United means everyone must be concerned about their place. There is pressure on all of us. Make no mistake, while we have a great squad there is a threat to all our places. At a club like this you have to be winning most weeks.'

In the wake of his international retirement, Real Madrid's superstar David Beckham sang the praises of his former teammate, as quoted in the *Liverpool Echo*. 'I played with Paul since we were 15 and he is one of his country's best ever players,' said the former Galáctico. 'I respect him as a person and a player and I wish him all the best.'

The decision to curtail his international career has left many wondering what might have been, but, with Scholes putting in commanding performances at club level in the twilight of his career, it is a decision that has benefited both player and club, as he has continued to perform at the highest level in a Manchester United shirt, despite being well into his thirties.

'It's always nice to have that ten-day break when the internationals come,' Scholes told the *Sunday Times* in 2007, three years after his international retirement. 'You do manage to get a nice rest. I would like to think I could play a bit longer than if I was playing for England.'

But the United midfielder admits he has been tempted to return to the international fold, as he told the *Manchester Evening News*: 'I reconsidered in 2006, but I am too old now – so there is no chance, sorry.'

Former Manchester United assistant manager Steve McClaren was well aware of Scholes's talents and, having worked with the player before, launched a new bid to bring him back to the national side when he took over after the 2006 World Cup in Germany.

'I spoke to Steve McClaren,' Scholes told the *Daily Mail*, 'but I thought I had got my form back playing for Manchester United and didn't want to do anything to jeopardise that. There are good players in the England team and they are always putting effort in, but for some reason it doesn't seem to click. I thought about it a lot because when the England manager rings, you should think about it.

'I spoke to Sir Alex Ferguson quite a lot and decided that I had probably done the right thing and didn't really want to go back. I am glad I made that decision. I have felt better for the rest you get when international football is being played. In tournament years, I might only get three weeks off, and that was tiring. As you get older, you tend to realise how lucky you have been to play football. I want to enjoy these last few years. Besides, I spend more time at home and, for me, there is nowhere better than Manchester.'

In summer 2007 Scholes was well and truly considered one of the elder statesmen at Old Trafford, and can benefit from his experience when looking at the new crop of youngsters there. 'I love playing in a side that can rip other teams apart,' he continued. 'The young lads are full of energy and talent. They are just happy all the time, not like us old gits! I have been lucky enough to win the league and hopefully I will win it again another couple of times. The international retirement helped me because I have come back refreshed. I hope it will prolong my career. Time will tell.'

Many had attributed Scholes's decision to quit to Eriksson's insistence on playing him out of position, but Scholes was keen to quash those rumours. 'I hear I didn't like being stuck on the left, but that wasn't an issue,' he said. 'I wasn't enjoying playing for England in general.'

Manchester United have continued to reap the rewards of his decision, while England, for all their star players and big names, have been unable to gel in his absence. The 2006 World Cup ended in defeat at the hands of Portugal in another nail-biting penalty shoot-out, while failure to qualify for the European Championships in Austria and Switzerland marked a new low for the England national team.

The high-profile appointment of Italian tactician Fabio Capello at the end of 2007 did not stop the rumours of an England return for Scholes, with the former Real Madrid boss admitting the door would always be open. 'There are players that don't want to be a part of England like Paul Scholes and Jamie Carragher,' he told Sky Sports. 'They are very good players and the door is always open.'

Chapter 10

EVOLUTION

'And without question Scholes will give us another
couple of years at the top level.'
SIR ALEX FERGUSON

W hat does the future hold for one of the greatest midfield
stars of a generation? Scholes has hinted in the past that
a move to Oldham could be a possibility – while saying at other
times that he could never imagine himself playing for anyone
other than his beloved Reds. Regardless of what happens when
Scholes plays his last game for Manchester United, though, he
has admitted he will not miss the life of a footballer, which has
never been to his liking.

'In a way I'm looking forward to finishing and everything that
goes with it,' he said in July 2008. 'The only thing I will definitely
miss is the football. It's the general life of a footballer I suppose,'
he continued. 'People are just very invasive and always wanting
to know what you're going to do.'

If Scholes does decide to hang up his boots in 2010, it will coincide with Sir Alex Ferguson's impending retirement, should the Scottish master not choose another dramatic U-turn. 'At the moment I just think two years would be about right,' he said. 'I feel okay right now and as long as I feel okay then I'll carry on.'

Regardless of who is at the helm of the club, Scholes is confident the future of Manchester United is in safe hands. 'I'd think I've two years left at the most. I've got one year left on my current deal and hopefully I'll get another one, but it all depends on how you're feeling and how you're playing. It's an exciting time and a good time to be involved,' he said on the club's pre-season tour of South Africa going into the 2008–09 season. 'The young players coming through are only going to be better next year for the experience they've had. Everyone who came in to the team last year played a massive part in our achievements.'

But, when asked if United could repeat their Champions League heroics, Scholes admitted it would be difficult to retain the trophy, which few have ever managed. 'It's a big ask but I feel we can only go from strength to strength. It's one thing having the talent and doing it in training every day but you've got to do it where it matters. Thankfully, we have the players who can do that – young lads who really don't seemed to be fazed by anything. They're very confident and look forward to the big games.'

Ferguson echoed his sentiments, but admitted that, despite a wealth of young talent at his disposal, he would continue to look to the old guard to help steer United's next generation into the dominant force in world football. 'I think we have a good team,' he told the *Manchester Evening News*. 'But I think there is still some development to come. There are some young players who appeared last season that did very well but for periods showed their youthfulness by being inconsistent. Those young players will come on a bundle now.

'That triumph of winning the league and the Champions League can only help us and players like Anderson, Nani, Rooney and Ronaldo will emerge from that and be really top players for us. Nani and Anderson will improve and that is the reason we bought them, to replace Scholes and Giggs in the long term. Giggs is 34 now but with the way we can control the number of games he plays, he still gives us a bit of real quality. He won't play every game but if he gives me 25 games of real quality, which he can do because he has looked after himself, that can keep us at the forefront in terms of players who can decide matches. And without question Scholes will give us another couple of years at the top level.'

But with Real Madrid courting Cristiano Ronaldo throughout the summer after their Champions League success, Scholes said that any player wishing to leave Old Trafford had better be prepared for a step down. He said, 'If people fancy a move and a bit of money, then good luck to them. But, if they're at a club like United, I don't think they realise how lucky they are to be playing there. It's always a step down after United. There are obviously big clubs in the world but, while certain people think it might be a progression if they move somewhere else, I don't think it is.'

With a host of European and domestic honours to his name,

Scholes has remained a humble, generous and much-loved figure within Manchester United Football Club, the perfect antithesis to the money-hungry mercenaries who plague the modern game. Far from searching for the spotlight, Scholes shies away, eager to be with his young family. He said of the post-match celebrations in Moscow, 'I was at the party but not for long because I had the kids there. You think about winning trophies for maybe a day or two, but then it's gone.'

And he admits that the winner's medal he received in Barcelona almost a decade ago is a worthless trinket due to his suspension from the final. 'I got a medal in 1999 as part of the squad but I don't view myself as a double Champions League winner. You've got to play in the final for it to count.'

He also said he shared a certain amount of sympathy for Chelsea for the way they lost the final – on penalties. 'You just felt sorry for them to lose in such a way,' he continued. 'If it had happened to us, we would have been devastated. There was nothing you could say to them except go over to shake their hands.'

With a trophy cabinet that rivals the greatest players football has ever produced, it is only in the twilight years of his career that Scholes is getting the recognition he deserves. Often overlooked, and chastised after being played out of position for both club and country, Scholes has proved himself invaluable to his club, and is beginning to reap the rewards of two decades of loyal service at the world's greatest football club. What is for sure is that Ferguson will always turn to the wise old heads, the likes of Ryan Giggs, Gary Neville and Paul

Scholes, to pass on their success, the formula they created for dominating domestic football, and to pass on their knowledge to the younger generations. It is all about evolution.